YOUR NEXT
BIG THING

YOUR NEXT BIG THING

Creating Successful Business Ideas from Scratch

MATTHEW MOCKRIDGE

With a Foreword by Bill Mockridge

Mango Publishing

CORAL GABLES

Cover design: Florian Eckelmann (KEEN Holding) at Martin Zech Design
Layout & Design: Martin Zech Design, Bremen | www.martinzech.de

For permission requests, please contact the publisher at:
Mango Publishing Group
2850 S Douglas Road, 2nd Floor
Coral Gables, FL 33134 USA
info@mango.bz

For special orders, quantity sales, course adoptions and corporate sales, please
email the publisher at sales@mango.bz. For trade and wholesale sales, please
contact Ingram Publisher Services at customer.service@ingramcontent.com or
+1.800.509.4887.

Your Next Big Thing: Creating Successful Business Ideas from Scratch

Library of Congress Cataloging-in-Publication number: 2019944189
ISBN: (print) 978-1-64250-141-4, (ebook) 978-1-64250-142-1
BISAC category code BUSINESS & ECONOMICS / Entrepreneurship

Printed in the United States of America

TABLE OF CONTENTS

Foreword By Bill Mockridge   9
Introduction   15
How This Book Works   29
The System Behind the Chapters   32

1

10 Thoughts on Creativity   35
  1. Where Are Your Creative Ideas Coming From?   36
  2. Being Creative Means Discovering and Improving—Not Just Inventing!   40
  3. Can You Learn or Inherit Creativity?   44
  4. Must You Always Be An Expert?   46
  5. The Flash of Genius—Does It Actually Exist?   47
  6. Who Are Your Five?   48
  7. Ecosystem—Habitat/Workspace   50
  8. The Creative Brain and Your Biceps   56
  9. Your Team and Its Members   58
  10. Less Is More   67

2

My 10 Favorite Idea-Finding Tools   71
  1. $100 Per Day   72
  2. Go. Stop. Breathe. Go!   75
  3. Brainstorming, Mind Mapping, Etc.   77
  4. Divergent Vs. Convergent Thinking   80
  5. Five Perspectives   82
  6. Sleep Well!   84
  7. Write It Down   85
  8. Fifty Ideas / Many More Combinations   86
  9. Matthew's Creativity Cocktail Technique   88
  10. Expose Yourself to New Things!   93

3

My Favorite 10 Idea-Evaluation Tools   97
  1. Critics   98
  2. Potential Customers   99
  3. Systems Vs. Humans   100
  4. How Big Is the Problem That Will Be Solved?   104
  5. What Makes the Competition Better/Worse?   105
  6. The 3D Photo: Journey Five Years Into the Future!   106
  7. Start At 100!   107
  8. Your Creative Friend   108

9. Auditioning for Ideas   111
10. What Would It Cost You To Quit?   112

4
10 Tips for "Success Thoughts" That Generate Ideas and the Power to Implement Them   117
1. Flow and Meditation   119
2. Journal of Joy   121
3. Fitness   125
4. Nutrition   129
5. The Winner's Routine   136
6. The "Willpower" Muscle   143
7. You Get All the Things You Focus On   148
8. Smile   151
9. Shock Yourself!   151
10. Go Where Your Fear Is the Greatest!   153

5
10 Systems for World-Class Leadership   159
1. T-O-D-A-Y a Leader   161
2. What You Can Learn from Children   174
3. Let's Talk, But Really! How to Master Difficult Conversations   182
4. A 10 Over Your Head   186
5. What Does Excellence Mean to Our Team?   202
6. Flying Without Taking Off   204
7. Speaking (Yes, in Front of Groups)   210
8. Eyes on the Road   213
9. Why Leaders Eat Last   215
10. Leaders Followers = Exponential Growth   217

Afterword   227
Thank You!   229
About the Author   231

Foreword By Bill Mockridge

It's quite astonishing: shortly after a child is born, I get the feeling that this tiny little person, who just saw the light of day an hour ago, is already whole. Of course, I know that the education they receive, the environment they grow in, and—above all—the friends they make, will have a strong influence on their development, and yet, I can't get rid of the feeling that the personality of this little person is already defined.

So it was with my brother Matthew: his birth was fast and uncomplicated, and he seemed particularly wide awake and curious as an infant. He was already a "natural-born leader" in primary school, but instead of being the center of attention, he was more concerned with helping others, encouraging them, and putting them in the spotlight. That's why I wasn't surprised when he told me that he wanted to write a guide for young aspiring entrepreneurs to help them get on their way.

I advised him to keep the information brief and concise. I have been presented with many different projects in recent years, and quickly developed a tactic to distinguish good ideas from bad. I usually tell the other guy, "You have fifty-nine seconds to convince me." In other words: be short, energetic, and to the point. Whoever can do that has my undivided attention. Otherwise, they won't get anywhere with me. I'm firmly convinced that a lot of content is not as complicated as some people think, but the perceived complication resides in the way it is communicated. You can express simple things in a very complicated way and complicated things very simply. What matters is that you must be convincing and enthusiastic about your idea *and* convey it all in two sentences.

Bill and Matthew (with a full head of hair or "volles haar"), 1998

Thirty-four years ago, I was totally excited about an idea that completely changed my life. In the early 1980s, I wanted to introduce improvisational theater to Germany. Because of my stage experience in North America, I knew the craft very well, and I was ready to produce comedy shows all over Europe. Despite all this, the transition from artist to businessman was not an easy one. I had many questions that friends and colleagues tried to answer as best they could, but at every turn I seemed to lack business expertise. What would I have given at the time for a sound guide on entrepreneurship—one that offered brief and precise answers to my questions as well as solutions to my problems! I could have really used a set of rules to evaluate my project in the short, medium, and long term—a book that would help me put together an effective team that I could rely on and grow with.

With *Your Next Big Thing*, Matthew has succeeded in writing a well-founded (but also very hip) guide book for young entrepreneurs.

A more recent Bill and Matthew (Heute caps: Today, in caps), 2015

This book dismantles complicated facts into individual parts that are immediately understandable, manageable, and, most importantly, practical. Matthew's clearly organized and sensible structure for the book makes it a fantastic reference for when problems arise and solutions are needed. Here's what I did: I read it all in one go, and then I placed it on the shelf above my desk with a note saying, "Check this out more often!"

So, if you're an energetic young person with great ideas and with the dream of helping your company achieve resounding success in today's market, I simply can't recommend a better book than *Your Next Big Thing*. That's just how good it is!

I'm now looking forward to YOUR "next big thing"!

Dig in!

Bill Mockridge
Founder of the Springmaus Theather

LET THE SHOW
BEGIN

First Act: the cover of this book is designed in blue and red. Why? Because over the past decade an entire generation has been conditioned by Facebook to associate these colors with a "notification"—the joy of spotting something new. This kind of subconscious dopamine boost increases the pickup rate in a bookstore, or the click rate in an online shop. My thanks go out to Mark Zuckerberg: *"Thanks for turning me into a brain ninja, buddy!"*

STARTING
UP

You have my respect just for the fact that you're holding this book.
That tells me a lot about you: You want *more*. You are hungry. You
really want to make a difference—with more doing, less talking. That
inspires me, and I'm already a big fan of yours!

Introduction

It's always been thrilling for me to help others understand how things (particularly victories) work—to help them analyze a seemingly inexplicable success, break it down to its basic components, and understand the success enough to replicate the outcome. That is my passion.

In researching this book, I've used others' strategies and methods (along with my own proven and tested ideas) as variables in a series of formulas and systems derived from the recurring behavioral patterns that I have observed. I hope you'll let me be your translator and guide, so that together we may decipher the complexities of successful creativity. We'll make our way through this dense jungle, help you find your really good ideas, and develop your presently undiscovered abilities—on the way to your "next big thing"!

I'll lead you by the hand as we make this journey using sixty proven methods that will allow you to produce groundbreaking ideas and summon unexpected accomplishments—ones that may change your life forever, just as they have changed mine. Practical tactical tools, like those in Chapter 3, give you the ability to generate ideas instantly. (Imagine that!) In Chapter 4, you'll acquire a whole new mindset based on systematic "success thoughts" which'll rearrange your patterns of thinking, opening up entirely new perspectives. You'll see the world through new eyes!

Resist the temptation to skip some chapters because this book provides more than just simple tools; it is about a complete shift in your current perception. We'll reconfigure your brain's creative thinking to improve your efficiency and effectiveness. We'll examine your current way of thinking and we'll look at how your thought patterns function. We'll help you focus on the right things, the right way. By the end of this book, you will be able to see opportunities, novel ideas, and potentials where others find only problems. And it will happen automatically, without too much practice. Imagine all the incredible places that a single, really good idea can take you! How will you feel when you discover that you can pull things out of your hat like a magician, leaving people delighted and amazed? This is the journey of your life—as a human being, and as an entrepreneur!

You might think that you lack creativity, are unable to learn, or are incapable of getting good ideas. In truth, that's the way most people think about themselves, so don't worry! You should read this book because *Your Next Big Thing* is not just about ideas; it affects all parts of your being. Everyone should learn the strategies that help discover one's best life and identify their capabilities, not unlike how a world-class boxer learns to use their fists. In the course of this book, I will present you with densely concentrated knowledge and powerful theories. I'll do this because I want you to quickly learn a series of practical action steps. I want you to learn these strategies and tactics the way a boxer finesses his fighting style, step-by-step, one maneuver at a time—left jab, right jab, uppercut, straight punch, left hook, right hook, and so on. You'll gradually become the Muhammad Ali of your own personal development. Consciously incorporate each new strategy into your routine and allow the new processes time to set in, becoming a part of what you do and who you are. You'll become a boxer who fights hard but keeps calm, who stands solidly but is still super fast. Learn every maneuver in peace and calmness, become one with your new knowledge. And don't rush it; give yourself time.

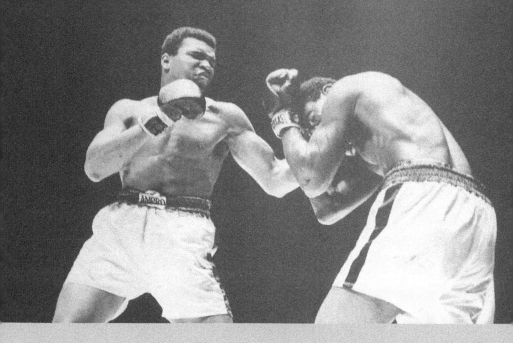

"FLOAT LIKE A BUTTERFLY,
STING LIKE A BEE."
—MUHAMMAD ALI

LIFE

You will learn how to live your best life and how this life can give you great business ideas!
Inventiveness and creativity in business are the products of a life that challenges you, that is fun and full of surprises, and that helps develop and fulfill you. The methods in this book serve to generate great entrepreneurial ideas, and they will, above all, help you establish a life bursting with adventure and inner fulfillment. Your next big idea starts with the next phase in your personal life, one full of new insights and perspectives. You will no longer identify with your "old life," and this totally new journey will make you truly happy.

LOVE

You will understand how a single idea can lead you to very special people, and how it can move your life forward!
Ideas are means of transportation. One single idea, one single new insight, can lead you to unexpected places, make your passion and zeal visible to others, and facilitate situations that you would otherwise never experience. In this newly found world, completely new acquaintances are waiting. Living your dreams is attractive; it balances you and helps you understand what you really need in life. It's a special blessing if you find a "significant other" while doing something you love; it guarantees an intersection of interests and values right from the start of the acquaintance.

BUSINESS

Your ideas will shape your business!
Creative ways of thinking are the neural highways and the traffic hubs for your success in business. You arrive at the business of your life via both right and wrong ideas. Regardless, life is an unforgettable journey. But a single idea completely changed my life as a man *and* a businessman.

FRIENDSHIP

You will become a friend to many!
Your business idea can connect people, both on your own team and within a target group. A single idea may explode into innumerable new social contacts. Your idea will become the motor of your social environment. As this environment of friendships and contacts evolves, so will you. Using the example of my story, and the underlying friendship between my three co-founders and me, we'll talk about the importance of those people that you truly let into your life.

FITNESS

You're going to get really strong!
Fitness means leading a life in which you maximize your physical and mental potential. Your business idea will only become as good as your physical assets can propel it. We'll look at the basic elements of really good, healthy fitness training, and we'll draw the unmistakable parallels between sports, creativity, and business. I've written this book since I not only want you to get in shape at your desk but also in the *rest* of your life!

HEALTH

Health is freedom! If you want more from life, you have to look after yourself more. Your health is the basis for every step, and enables the mental and temporal freedom you need to develop ingenious ideas.

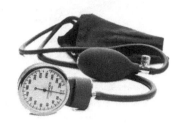

FINANCES

Money becomes a tool that you'll truly master! Without money, the best idea is no good, so we will take a close look at what happens to the money that flows into and out of your ideas. We'll set clear parameters and develop rules for healthy monetary growth.

TIME

Your days become unique. Once you understand how to truly live, time becomes your most valuable resource. Sure, you can earn back lost money, correct mistakes, and apologize to people. But you'll *never* get your time back. Wasted time shows the greatest disrespect to your own potential. To ensure that you get the maximum value per invested unit of time, I will summarize some effective productivity systems. But remember, sometimes the most productive thing to do is to pause (see Health).

THEN
AND
NOW

1986

Born in Bonn, Germany as the second of six boys. My parents are actors. Creativity and artistry are integral parts of my earliest childhood years.

Yup, that's me! (In German: „Yup, das bin ich!")

1993

I'm in grade school and sell the candy I collect during Halloween—a pretty sweet business model. My Italian grandmother takes over much of my upbringing, while my parents work long and hard. I come to understand the value of family, religion, and respect, and I observe the kind of authentic, independent work that makes dreams come true. Even today, I'll still call and visit my grandmother regularly—an indescribably good feeling.

1997

I attend an all-boy Catholic high school where I learn Latin. (WTF?!) Prayers before each class and mass every Tuesday. Sports are also very important. I learn discipline, order, diligence, pack mentality, and way too little math.

2000

I'm thirteen years old during the big mobile phone hype of the late '90s, so I try to import 800 super cheap phones from China to Germany using the money my grandma gave me for my First Communion (meant to go into my college savings fund). The phones never arrive. The money's gone. I close my import/export business and learn one of the most important entrepreneurial lessons: fall down, get back up, and *rethink everything*. So, I continue my research and find a supplier who actually delivers cheap cell phones. Although I don't buy anything (my communion money is gone), I understand that other aspiring entrepreneurs would like to make quick profits, so I sell the phone supplier's contact info to kids from the neighborhood. Suddenly I am getting real money for a piece of paper with an email address written on it. My entrepreneurial thinking changes forever.

2006

I graduate from high school with a primary focus on sports (one of my passions) and English (which I speak fluently, thanks to my Canadian father). I've hardly attended school during the last two years—not out of laziness, but rather pure efficiency: I optimized the inputs while still ensuring the right outcome.

2012

I finish my studies in international business and management in Miami, FL. The college system in the United States has been good to me—a really great experience. I've built two companies with my three best friends in my 140-square-foot college dorm. One of these companies is NEONSPLASH–Paint-Party®, a crazy idea that will later become our first real international success! Back then, we filled every bottle of paint ourselves. After graduation, I'm nominated for the Young Business Alumni "Hall of Fame" Award.

German Glossary
unterdruck: under pressure
Abfüllstutzen: filling station/filling nozzle

2014

New concepts have followed NEONSPLASH–Paint-Party®. We tour ZOMBIE RUN®, our zombie-themed 5 km obstacle course, and City Slide®, our 500 m urban waterslide, all across Europe. It seems as if one of our shows is taking place every weekend, somewhere on the continent. From Ibiza to Amsterdam, our guests experience unforgettable moments. My co-founders and I live together. We work hard, travel often, laugh a lot, and live our dream!

2019

I've been asked repeatedly: "How does it work? How do I get to live your life?" So, now I'm sitting down and writing a book.

MATTHEW'S Q&A

- **What few people know:** I always take ice-cold showers.

- **Favorite music:** Depends on the situation. At the gym—electronic. For work/focus—classical or binaural beats. In the shower—'90s Pop. Driving, walking, or cooking—audiobook/podcast.

- **Food:** healthy (sushi/Thai/salad/Italian)

- **Vacation:** Muskoka, Canada

- **Coke or Pepsi:** none, just water

- **Weakness:** Difficulty saying "no" to new business opportunities. I've learned something important along the way: If it's not a "hell, yes," it's a "no!" (Thanks, Derek Sivers.)

- **Strength:** Discipline. I've never been the best/most intelligent/strongest /most talented, but I always work harder and more consistently than expected. My advice—create winning habits!

- **Proudest Moment as an Entrepreneur:** Knowing when I've done enough.

- **Aha! Moment:** When life blossoms from the inside out.

- **Best Advice:** Help your dreams and those of others come true.

- **Favorite Book:** *Tao Te Ching* by Laozi

- **Favorite Film:** *The Little Prince*

- **Favorite Quote:** 'Be the change you wish to see in the world." (Gandhi)

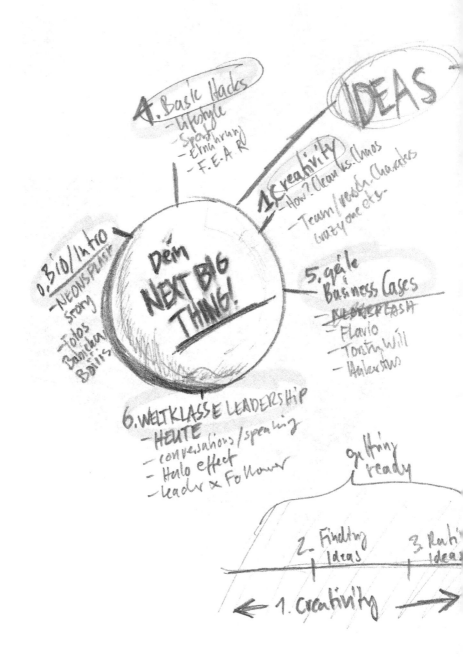

IDEAS

4. Basic Hacks
- Lifestyle
- Sporthrun)
- Ernährung
- F.E.A.R

1. Creativity
- How? Clean vs. Chaos
- Team/reach. Charakters
- crazy one etc.

0. 3'10/Intro
- NEONSPLASH
- Story
- Fotos
- Bamberg
- Basics

Dein
NEXT BIG
THING!

5. geile
Business Cases
- NEONSPLASH
- Flavio
- Tonsty Will
- Halvestus

6. WELTKLASSE LEADERSHIP
- HEUTE
- conversations/speaking
- Halo effect
- Leadr x Follower

getting
ready

2. Finding
Ideas

3. Rati
Ideas

← 1. creativity →

26

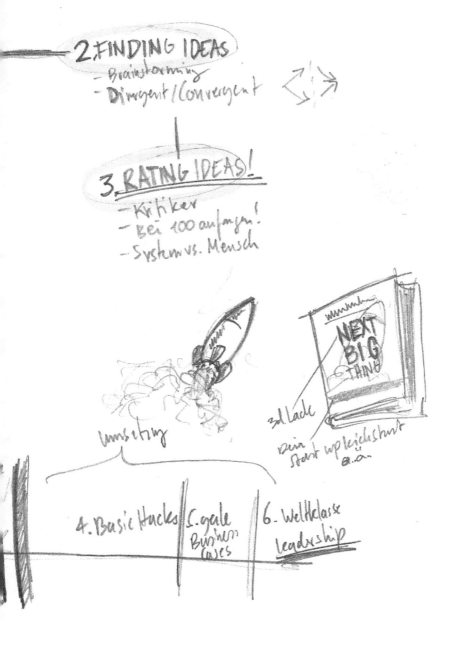

2. FINDING IDEAS
- Brainstorming
- Divergent / Convergent

3. RATING IDEAS!
- Kritiker
- Bei 100 anfangen!
- System vs. Mensch

NEXT BIG THING

3d Lack
Dein Start up gleich stark
@...

Umsetzung

4. Basic Hacks | 5. geile Business Cases | 6. Weltklasse Leadership

How This Book Works

I focus on two principles to guide you to success: Substance and Practicality.

This book is intended to help you generate the highest return on investment (ROI) in terms of time and money, and as quickly as possible. During the research for this book, I was inspired by two basic theories of physics—to create optimal "Stability" (or "Substance") and "Impact" (or "Practicality").

I had a clear conceptual vision while writing this book: I wanted to structure it in a way that I, as a reader myself, would enjoy it. I usually prefer to absorb knowledge in short bursts; I prefer short articles or chapters, as opposed to long passages. Because of my passion for systemization, efficiency, and high-leveraging, I focused on the Pareto Principle, also known as the 80/20 rule: "Which 20 percent of my experience is responsible for 80 percent of my success?" (More on that later.) In other words: "What is the essential?" When I listen to (short) interviews with experts, I expect dense content, and I'm interested in the essentials. I conceived *Your Next Big Thing* as a collection of important and clearly structured ideas and action steps—no fluff and no confusion. This structure was a no-brainer for me.

Let's go back to our basic principles: Stability and Impact. I wanted this book to "be like a nail"!

Wait… *a nail?!* Let me explain.

(I have attached a definition of the word "nail" to the end of this chapter in case you are unfamiliar with it.)

STABILITY

Imagine an old fakir lying on a bed of nails. Why do none of the sharp tips pierce his skin? Because his weight on the board is evenly distributed. Through distribution, the pressure is relieved, redistributed, and the danger averted. Tada! Similarly, the information contained in this book is organized in a way that keeps you from being overwhelmed by the incisive ideas needed to bring your most brilliant ideas to fruition. Although every idea in this book is important (sharp), what makes it work is the arrangement of these ideas (the nails), which together create a truly stable platform. Confusion becomes clarity, and to your enthralled audience, you become a seemingly invulnerable fakir, with fascinating magical tricks.

IMPACT

Carefully chosen and properly arranged, the individual "nails" of this book are indispensable tools for constructing your most creative work—and your best life. The ideas I share allow you to cut through the fog, use your resources to create new structures, and break the status quo. These ideas are both the foundation and the results of any endeavor. Together, nail-by-nail, you and I will examine the structure of success, back to its logical source. Every method in this book helps you construct "your next big thing." Our examination of your inner life will change your perspective forever.

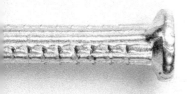

Nail
/nāl/
noun

A small metal spike with a broadened flat head, driven typically into wood with a hammer to join things together or to serve as a peg or hook.

WHAT IS A "NEXT BIG THING"?

Before you can understand how to develop your "next big thing," I should first clarify what attributes make something a truly "next big thing." We will use those attributes (or values) as a guide or checklist when considering different proposals. A real "next big thing" includes all or some of the following features:

MEANING/VALUE

A real "next big thing" costs time, energy, and attention. It becomes an integral part of its founder's life, and is closely connected to a team, an environment, customers, and partners. Questioning the meaning and value of the "next big thing" opens the dialogue about the conviction (the "why"), and the vision that form its foundation. In any company, the emotional appeal of a project (the "BIG" in "next big thing") is missing unless there are enduring values and "real" meaning.

FAIRNESS

Right is right, and wrong is wrong. A real "next big thing" must consider the principles of morality and ethics—whether it's legal, fair, and honest.

PROBLEM-SOLVING

Big problems set the stage for big ideas. How big is the question that will be answered? How big is the problem that will be solved? Your next big problem will open up a market that has big potential.

SCALABILITY

A true "next big thing" is always bigger than the single brain behind it. Can the idea really scale, function, and grow, even without the founder standing next to it? Scaling-up creates exponential growth and paves the way for long journeys.

OPTIMIZED RISK

The market rewards risk and brilliance. A smart "next big thing" generates profits inversely proportional to the risk. A true "next big thing" is smart, doesn't financially paralyze you, and clearly tells you when to collect your chips and leave the table.

The System Behind the Chapters

Read the table of contents like a blueprint. It is a set of systematic building instructions for successfully constructing your next big idea. An important note: only one of the five chapters deals with the brainstorming process. Of course, your brainstormed idea sets the foundation of your "next big thing," but you need all the other chapters to build on that foundation. Imagine that you are building a house:

The first chapter, with its ten thoughts on creativity, deals with the mechanics behind your vision. There's no house yet—just a plot and a vision. The more clearly defined your vision is, the more likely your house will fulfill you in every detail. It is an art to have visions, and not everyone can see them.

2 The second chapter presents ten practical tools for brainstorming and finding ideas to help you design your house. You will create the plans and technical drawings, evaluate all the material requirements, and create the (theoretical) foundation of your house.

3 The third chapter provides ten tools for evaluating ideas: your construction plans will be checked by "structural engineers" with tests on safety, stability, durability, efficiency, and common sense. If your plans pass our inspection, your house will be structurally sound.

4 The fourth chapter introduces ten success-focused ideas for powerful implementation. It will guide you through the construction phase of your house. You will learn how to lay the foundation and set the first bricks so that your vision can become reality.

5 The fifth chapter provides ten thoughts on world-class leadership that will transform you from simple homeowner into full-blown winner in the game of the best version of your life. Your vision has been realized, and your plans fulfilled: your house is standing and it's filled with great people who inspire you. Now the task is about having a household that not only works, but is also fun and fulfilling, bringing many happy moments to you and everyone else involved.

10 THOUGHTS ON
CREATIVITY

Okay, you may be thinking: "But I'm not creative at all!" An important thought before we go out on the thin ice of creativity together: Creativity is not so much a skill. It's an *attitude*, and ultimately an evaluation made by the beholder. And as an evaluation, creativity comes *after* the creation.

An artist will throw four shades of yellow on a canvas and sell the thing for ten million dollars. Why? Because someone decided it was unbelievably creative. Which came first, the creation or that evaluation?

Let's follow this train of thought for a moment. What would happen if we disregarded our nervousness and uncertainty about our own creativity, and only concentrated on the one element of the creative process that we can control, our action? So, in this chapter, we'll disassemble creativity and—from now on—focus only on the nails we can sink.

The following ten thoughts about creativity are actionable and foolproof, contrarily to whatever you might hear from art gallery small talk. Start before you're ready! Creativity can only be confirmed after you've made the first brush stroke. Claim your creativity by just getting started! To believe in your gift, your talent, the artistry of your next really great idea—*that* is the true creativity, and that's what will uncover your genius. Just between us: creativity is, above all, a synonym for courage. Let's walk out onto the thin ice together! Let me help you grab hold of your courage and show the world your art—one step at a time!

1. WHERE ARE YOUR CREATIVE IDEAS COMING FROM?

We'd made it! We (my three best friends and co-founders, Flo, David, Siamak—and I) were beaming: our entrepreneurial dream had come true! One hour before our fourth NEONSPLASH–Paint-Party® event, more than 5,000 guests lined up outside the door, waiting to be let into the sold-out concert hall. They came to dance to electronic music and get hit with neon paint balls. Something that, at the time, might have seemed unimaginable, and even offensive, became my first really successful business idea.

Our business idea worked, and it worked really well. More than 500,000 people have visited us to date in more than 60 cities throughout Europe. And they would readily agree. "The best party of my life," is what most say after a NEONSPLASH–Paint-Party®.

I'm often asked how we got the idea. My answer is short and honest: "We didn't come up with the idea; the idea came up to us!" Ideas come from the sum of everything you are exposed to—they are the product of your environment. Can you stay home and generate good ideas just by typing on your computer? Forget it! But go for a walk, talk to new people, read books that challenge you, and visit new places, and you won't be able to save yourself from good ideas.

Fact: change yields progress. The average tenure at ultra-creative companies like Google is just over one year. Why? Because constant change promotes continual evolution. There's a correlation between change and development. If the local bank down the street has been pursuing the same strategy for thirty years, this is certainly because the same heads have been sitting in meetings for thirty years. If the implementation of new ideas is related to the turnover of employees (and the new thoughts that new employees bring), then Google develops at a rate thirty times faster than the local bank. (In reality, it's many times more.)

So, back to summer 2008—my first year at a typical U.S. university in Tampa, Florida. My buddy David and I love the new life at school (and the beach) and are realizing our version of the American Dream. We're tens of thousands of kilometers away from home, from everything we know and understand. We are vulnerable, not always fully in control, and those are important ingredients for modesty and honesty.

Still, we don't know our way around; we're often lost or disoriented, and have to ask for directions. But it is specifically the things that we don't yet know that are going to lay the foundation of our entrepreneurial success.

CHANGE YIELDS PROGRESS!

It's a typical Saturday evening, but still somewhat special: A student fraternity invites us to a "Blacklight Paint Party," where all the light bulbs have been changed to blacklight. Everyone will paint colorful quotes, names, and whatnot on each other's t-shirts. Sounds weird and crazy, so David and I say, "We're in!" The experience will change our lives forever. As the night progresses, the painting becomes messier and messier, but the vibe is indescribably special: it's a hit! The music is loud, the air sizzling, and even though there's little space for the few hundred people to dance, everyone—but really, *every single one*—feels that something extraordinary is happening. The organized painting has been forgotten, and everyone is smearing each other with paint. There are no taboos, flirting has never been so easy, and interaction has never been so high.

A supercharged version of a party game for young adults had emerged and was unstoppable.

And that's what matters! An absolute parade of an idea drove past me, with sirens and flashing lights, certainly still very raw and unstructured, but obvious! And it was happening, not because I was so creative, but because I was in the right place at the right time. Whoever doesn't jump on a chance like that—it's their own fault.

The lesson is that you don't come up with ideas like that, they come to you! You have to loosen your cognitive dependencies and be open to what would normally be impossible. Always question conventional logic, paint big pictures, and create your own reality—without boundaries.

Like a camera lens, I try to zoom out far and see everything in the long shot. I try to see things not for what they are, but for what they could be. I look at the party crowd, feel the energy that makes the room tremble, and the mental machine starts running. I don't imagine a few hundred guests, but instead 5,000—a stage, a show, and a countdown, like on New Year's Eve, until the first color hits. I sense a theme and tour. My head spins and I realize: *This is the next big thing!*

2. BEING CREATIVE MEANS DISCOVERING AND IMPROVING—NOT JUST INVENTING!

After the Blacklight Paint Party, the task was clear: I had a basic idea that I had to improve upon or amplify. But how? Creativity does not automatically mean inventing something new; it often simply means discovering something and then making proper use of it. Ideas always build on each other; they're much more evolutionary than revolutionary. Our first really successful idea, NEONSPLASH–Paint-Party®, already had its parameters defined: color, music, and blacklight. So now it became all about amplifying the concept, finding new elements and adding them to the basic idea, and about challenging the conventional wisdom about entertainment. Do you have to reinvent the wheel? No, but it has to roll, and roll really fast!

DISCOVERY: COLOR IS THE HIGHLIGHT!

HOW WE IMPROVED IT: We added a dramatic story arc, defining a framework for action—a countdown, just like on New Year's Eve. At the end of a two-hour countdown, the color would burst off the stage for the first time!

DISCOVERY: T-SHIRTS

HOW WE IMPROVED IT: White t-shirts became obligatory for all guests, for two reasons:

1. Neon color looks very strong on white t-shirts.

2. We dress the guests like a team; they look like they're wearing team jerseys, so to speak. The sense of community is enhanced.

DISCOVERY: GOOD SHOW BUT NO NAME

HOW WE IMPROVED IT: We frame each show by creating its own title, story, and message, just like in the world of cinema or big concert tours. Why? Because people love stories, and because stories bring life to otherwise generic activities. So, in 2011, we did the *Love Thru Paint* tour, in 2012/13 the *Color Is Creation* tour, and in 2014 the *Utopia 3D* tour (with 3D red-and-blue paper glasses reminiscent of 90s movies, and 3D image effects on screen). All of the events had the same basic elements: color, music, blacklight. But every show had a new story, and a new reason to participate. And as an added draw, we used a big stage, intricate effects, and famous artists.

We identified the characteristics of extremely successful and exceptional events, incorporated them into our basic idea, and thereby created a new hybrid that really has it all. Applied creative thinking is, therefore, not a process of invention, but rather the systematic identification and the atypical combination of past experiences to create entirely new configurations. In the right setting, these can produce results that are not just successful, but also groundbreaking hits.

In his book *Tipping Point*, Malcolm Gladwell talks about how trending new developments reach a point of instability, after which the situation rapidly readjusts. Using the example of a completely full glass of water into which additional drops of water are added, Gladwell points out how the extra water will mound up above the rim until the "tipping point" is reached, the moment when the mound of water collapses and overflows.

We can view each drop as a player entering the new market, reacting to the enticing promise of a really good novel idea. The mass of new entrants builds up beyond what the glass can normally hold, until the surface tension breaks and most of the excess water spills over. At that point, the new trend becomes an integral part of a market, though it's essential not to get washed away in the floods. Only a few survive all the way to the "tipping point," and even fewer survive the wash-out and go on to dominate the entire segment. The few companies that manage have a very clear vision right from the first drop, and analyze the dynamics so precisely that they start the challenge with increased stability and reason for being.

Let's take another concrete example: Amazon. Today, it's a player in the e-commerce segment, and probably only at the beginning of its world domination. Let's consider for a moment what founder Jeff Bezos noticed and expanded on in 1994 (!). What did the "glass" of the e-commerce market look like back then, and what happened? Let's put ourselves in his shoes (surely Converse Chucks, before they became cool for the third time): He recognized the growth and infinite potential of the Internet and decided to sell things online. He created a framework, an interface that could carry and transmit his idea, at a time when the playing field for his idea (the "glass") was still not overfilled with players. But consider: How did Jeff Bezos deal with this new e-commerce opportunity?

Where would Amazon be today if Jeff Bezos had decided to use this "new Internet" to sell fresh fruit? Nowhere. (Nothing against the currently numerous startups in the fresh fruit/food delivery niche.)

But books were an exciting product for his new idea. Why? Because you don't have to physically touch a book to make a purchase decision. Considering the opposite market, I prefer to know the condition of a banana before I buy it. I want to touch it—is it mushy or not? You don't necessarily have to touch a new book. Another killer attribute that Bezos found: books have an abundant variety. They are innumerably different, and Amazon can offer them all because the company doesn't have to physically own them, which instantly made Amazon the biggest bookstore in the world. And the kicker: it can sell cheaper because the fixed costs are lower, and the target group much larger. So, Bezos traded the in-store customer's ability to handle the product and immediately take possession for the minimized transaction costs (no one has to go to the bookstore anymore), a broader choice, and (in many countries) a better price. At the present, Shopify and other tools are helping players from all over the world "drip" into the e-commerce market, and the excess water has been building up in the "glass" of e-commerce, but when it collapses, Bezos is better positioned than the others—he's ready to ride the wash-out, and survive.

So, find existing opportunities, rearrange them and improve them! The competition will follow, drop by drop. The only important thing is to be one of the drops that survive!

3. CAN YOU LEARN OR INHERIT CREATIVITY?

Creativity is an attitude, much more than it is a skill. In most cases, the product of creativity (the idea) results from numerous experiments and effective evaluations. My grandmother always said: "Throw 100 things in the air; something will eventually stick!" No mystery about the creative genius of billionaire James Dyson. He built 5,126 vacuum cleaner prototypes over the span of fifteen years before his cyclone technology became a global phenomenon. Teresa Amabile of Harvard Business School writes that creativity is too often confused with expertise. We usually don't see the years of work and the incessant trial-and-error that's often required to create a masterpiece.

Creativity is neither inherited, nor is it learned by rote, like the ABCs. There are other models and exercises, besides "Matthew's Ten Favorite Idea-Finding Tools," that can stimulate or guide you in finding creative ideas, but these are like the handrail in a stairwell: you still have to climb the stairs yourself. Creativity is not the wine, but the vine that connects the rain and the storm with the sun and the soil. The vine variety is selected by the vintner, and its growth is influenced by where it is planted. Give the vine what it needs. Encourage it!

When you experience something unfamiliar, your brain works at unimaginable speed, and a huge network of neurons seek to interpret the experience. If that experience repeats itself, the memory needs to activate significantly fewer neurons. But also remember to break away from relying on old experiences and on linear thinking!

FIRST STEP: SELL YOUR TV!

When watching television, the brain operates primarily in a passive state, kind of an "awake sleep." Your brain must be active and stimulated before it can begin the complex thought processes that require an elevated level of alpha waves (reading/writing/movement).

SECOND STEP: NO PHONES!

Switch to "airplane mode," and your productivity, creativity and general focus will increase significantly. I lost my mobile phone in a taxi in Amsterdam and was surprised at how good life felt without it. Ask yourself how many of your calls are actually productive, enjoyable and indispensable! Texting and playing also rob us of focus. While my phone was lost, I made my important calls over Skype (you can also use it to call phones and mobiles) and was faster and more productive than with a mobile phone. Lose your phone and suddenly your actions become more purposeful: You don't simply react to external stimuli (your cellphone's ringtone tearing you away from everything else). You become more committed to the present and you think ahead much better. You are more likely to arrive on time for meetings and you are more aware of the relevance of each conversation. Try it!

Let yourself be surprised! You don't always need to know what will happen next; you don't always need to be fully prepared and qualified. Let your brain work with more imagination, commitment and creativity.

Not everyone is born creative, but every person you encounter, every setting or situation you experience, can set in motion creative thinking. Expose yourself to unfamiliar situations—the crazier, newer, sharper, and more drastic the experience, the more innovative the ideas will result in being. Don't be afraid to astound yourself and everyone around you. Watch what happens!

4. MUST YOU ALWAYS BE AN EXPERT?

Repetition creates experience, and over many years, becomes the basis of true expertise. But expertise comes with a price: a potentially rigid understanding. Could it be that a high expertise correlates with decreased flexibility and imagination? When do experience, knowledge, and biased perception begin to hinder truly innovative approaches?

In his book, *The Myths of Creativity*, David Burkus tells the story of prosthesis manufacturer Martin Bionics. Its founder, Jay Martin, fired an entire staff of the most experienced, best-paid doctors and physicians because they declared that a real time responsive ankle prosthesis was technically impossible. In their place, he created a research team of mere students—students who were already experienced enough to understand complex relationships, but fresh enough not to rule out the seemingly impossible. He expected these students to see his vision through to the end. And after just a few months, Jay Martin and his team of students successfully completed the project and developed the unthinkable: an ankle replacement that revolutionized the prosthetic market.

Creativity does not result from an expert performing a miracle, but from a design "ecosystem" based on the right team and on a mix of perspectives, new and old. Not knowing that something is impossible makes it once again possible!

5. THE FLASH OF GENIUS—DOES IT ACTUALLY EXIST?

Suddenly, out of nowhere, a winning idea! Stories about the "flash of genius"—of accidental inspiration and sudden ingenuity—are widespread. Everybody is familiar with the cartoon symbolism of the light bulb, flashing above a person's head like lightning. The idea seemingly arrives at the speed of light. Apparently a million-dollar moment—but what is missing? All the considerations that led to the "aha!" moment.

The efforts that preceded the insight are often overlooked. Why? Because they are often invisible—nobody sees, hears, feels, or understands the toils and the subconscious incubation of an idea. The subconscious part of our mind processes thoughts millions of times faster than the conscious part, and the subconscious creation of ideas occurs in a sphere that is completely different than the one used for everyday actions. It functions while sleeping, showering, and when going for a walk. People do not notice the internal mental interplay of impressions and inspirations that allows the idea to take shape. They only see what emerges: the success story, or well-formed idea.

Even though the "flash of inspiration" concept has long been scientifically refuted, people still love the story and want to believe in it. Why? Because it's a wonderful excuse for anyone who believes that they are not creative and don't have good ideas. It makes it easy to avoid trying. Unfortunately, if capable people don't at least pretend to believe in the "flash of inspiration," really good ideas may actually fail to materialize.

The recipe for brainstorming winning ideas requires not only working directly on the main idea, but also subconscious processing, conviction, patience, serenity, distance, and being open to new impressions. The greatest artists and thinkers (da Vinci, Michelangelo, and similar people) have always had many projects and gigs going on at the same time, even while focusing on the project of the moment. What might seem at first glance to be excessive or lacking in structure, is likely being further processed, incubated, and driven on the subconscious level. Sooner or later, the moment comes when the idea is mature— many people incorrectly interpret that moment as a "flash of genius." The actual idea, however, arrived via an incubation process. A new impetus has emerged, a new path is being taken, and additional new ideas and approaches will naturally follow.

6. WHO ARE YOUR FIVE?

Ideas are products of our environment; we've already established that. Our direct environment and the people who are closest to us are another variable that has an effect on the emergence of our ideas because these people inspire us, shape our views, and determine our way of thinking. Everything we think possible, our beliefs and imagination, our understanding about possibilities and potential, are the result of our social interactions. The careful and cautious selection of "The Five," the members of your inner circle, your closest allies, your team of companions, sets the needed foundation for your creativity.

What are the criteria for joining this team? Who can play with you? Are there different team positions, or are all five going to be forwards? Before you start placing players on the field, consider the overall mindset. What does this team believe in, what does it want to achieve, and why? Your five closest advisors will create an ecosystem. The culture within this ecosystem will set the mood in the locker room before the big game, and determine how engaged they get in the huddle, and how loud they chant.

The Five will always act with conviction.

And with conviction comes will—the will of each individual to become the best at what inspires their participation on the team. Wanting to be the best helps prevent limited vision and conflict.

The Five expect each other to become world-class achievers in what they're passionate about and intend to always help each other. This conviction creates a force that everyone can feel. There's no jealousy, only a real desire for each of your friends to have more.

With conviction also comes a pure truth—as clean, as clear, and as refreshing as an icy mountain lake. A kind of truth that is so sudden and so immediate that it often hurts. There are no more doubts because they have each other's word. They interact with blind trust and with unspoken understanding when it's game time. The ideas and the favorable situations they create may look like magic to the outsiders sitting at the stadium. But for these five, it's just a game played with passion and real drive, a game that focuses effort toward the same cause with a passion toward the team as a whole, and a game played with enthusiasm for each of its players. The world watches in amazement as these five outplay their opponents. The strength of these five comrades really lies in the heart of each player and in the group hug shared in the locker room after the winning point. But only the members of this innermost circle will see and understand that point.

THE FIVE OF YOUR FIVE

Each of your "five" also deserves their own team of allies. (And who are the other five of each of your five?) Your indirect environment has an influence on you. You immediately sense when one of your five is happy—it also makes you happy and affects your well-being. You can now pass this new energy on to other people in your direct environment. If we follow these connections, it becomes clear that your energy, your well-being, your productivity, and your success, are also affected by all indirect environments—the five of your five, and of each of their respective fives, etc. Human happiness is never only the result of a one-dimensional interaction, but also the product of the dynamics of all social contacts, across multiple levels. The entire social network influences your decisions. If a friend of a friend smokes, it could increase the chance that you could become a smoker.

So, choose these five carefully, and encourage them to choose their five well, and encourage their five…Well, you get the idea.

7. ECOSYSTEM—HABITAT/WORKSPACE

How does it feel when you sit at your desk? Are you really inspired when you're there? Does your workspace bring out the best in you, open you up to your greatest ideas and visions, motivate you to go beyond yourself, and live the best version of your life?

The correlation between space and performance has long been known. In his book, *Back to a Future for Mankind*, Dr. Ibrahim Karim presents the concept of biogeometry. According to his research, the architecture of rooms and their furniture have a considerable influence on the occupants' energy, harmony, and vitality. Not concerned with the immeasurable spiritual vibe of a place, his studies focus instead on scientifically verifiable results regarding the effect of spaces on people. Experiments prove that pictures on the wall have the potential to produce higher concentrations of serotonin than any chemical drug. Paying attention to the physical environment can be extremely important because of its potential to optimize our work. Because we spend so much time in the office, we owe it to ourselves—and to our potential—to use this time efficiently! Creating an inspiring living and working space is fortunately not so difficult.

MY FIVE TIPS

ORDER

Order brings focus and sharpens the senses. Order is structure and boosts productivity. Pieces of paper just lying around with no specific places for them affect both clarity and structure. This means that all documents, all pieces of mail, and all other "stuff" are best handled immediately. Don't put it off. Smart office tools—such as hanging files—should not be piled up, but instead hung in a row, arranged and neatly labeled. In psychology, the Zeigarnik effect states that we tend to remember open tasks more than completed ones. This means that any unfinished task remains in the back of your mind and sucks precious resources. The same applies to your desktop, calendar and email inbox.

Very important: if you have a lot of email, rather than trying to handle it in one sitting, it may be better to divide the task into manageable sessions. For instance, after 90 minutes, take a 10- to 20-minute break—go for a walk, eat something, have a conversation. Then return fresh and continue.

QUICK TIP

Sign one-way emails with "NRN" (no response necessary), so that your mailbox is not full of answers like yes / thank you / okay / cool, etc.

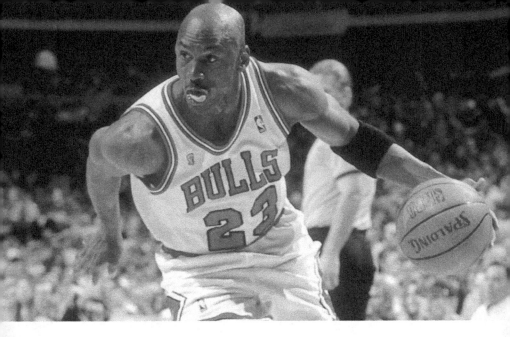

PICTURES

Photos and decorative pictures create visions. They create escape spaces and inspiration. They stimulate and connect you with the emotions of your choice.

As I'm writing this chapter, I have a few photos on my desk: my wife and daughter, my parents and family, Michael Jordan in tears, clutching the NBA Championship Cup, and my business partners.

Yes, Michael Jordan.

Pictures push emotional buttons. They transport us to other worlds, give us security and strength, and represent our feelings. Even a quick glance at them creates a healthy break, providing strength and support. The eyes are the windows to the soul. It's not just what you see, but also what moves you. Let only beautiful images into your soul—things that make you joyful, proud, and happy. Every picture is worth more than a thousand words.

KITCHEN

While I attended house parties in college, it quickly became clear to me that the best part of the party happens in the kitchen! And even today in our office, the kitchen is still an important hub—a kind of control center. But why? The kitchen is informal. The usual laws of the desk do not apply. Here, you're just one hungry human being. Since you can have normal conversations and decompress, suddenly the expectations drop. Yet, these are all important prerequisites for relaxed thinking and getting fresh impressions.

Cooking, you create a break in your routine by give yourself a new environment and a new task. You're here for dinner, and for a moment you allow your gaze to turn away from the unsolvable task of the day. But then, suddenly, the solution comes to you.

The potential of the kitchen is enormous, multiplied many times over if it is also filled with the right ingredients. I recommend fresh fruit and vegetables, lots of water (best to get a fridge with a water dispenser), fish (smoked salmon tastes great, is healthy, and is ready to eat), protein powder (for the body builders), whole grain bread, freshly squeezed juices, and nuts or trail mix. It's best to eat together as a team as often as possible, to laugh, to have good conversations, and enjoy the partnership. The kitchen always provides a good opportunity to define and strengthen the culture of the company and the philosophy of the team.

LIGHT

I don't like hospital-style fluorescent tubes that try to imitate daylight, but instead look sterile and boring. Lots of real daylight, bright wall colors, and decorating with warm tones create a more pleasant atmosphere.

What can you do to keep you and your team in the office as long as possible? Put another way: What would you do to prepare your apartment for a nice date? Right! Clean up and create the proper, pleasant atmosphere. It has to be cozy and beautiful, pleasant and inspiring. In our office, we have floor-to-ceiling windows, a large roof terrace, warm light sources, and soft ceiling floodlights, as well as colored LED lights. Concerts, festivals, and clubs create their very own worlds just by using concepts in lighting. So, make it nice and you'll enjoy being in the office. Soon you'll associate positive emotions with your work!

CULTURE

What does your workplace stand for? What are the foundational values of your team? Your philosophy, mission, leadership, interaction, and ethics are the emotional furnishings of your workplace. What does your workplace culture feel like? Is it rather sterile and flat? Is it cozy and warm? Or is it just a little bit different?

A fulfilled person, a strong team, and a successful company all have a clear vision, share it a lot and openly, and do everything they need to fulfill their dreams. Members of a strong team trust each other blindly, share the shirts off their back, agree on fundamental principles, and share a common passion and faith—all this they do so harmoniously that an unstoppable energy arises. They resonate with each other. You can recognize their will to win, see it flashing in their eyes, and feel it in every handshake.

My tip for a better corporate culture—or just for you to create more meaning for yourself in the daily craziness of building your dreams—is to *ask some good questions!*

Ask good questions, get good answers, and change the spirit of your environment in minutes!

WHAT DO WE STAND FOR?

WHAT DO WE WANT?

HOW DO WE GET THERE?

HOW SHOULD OTHERS SEE US?

WHAT DO WE NOT WANT?

OFFENSE INSTEAD OF DEFENSE

We are on the road a lot. I live and work in countless cities—both because of our events and my work as a speaker—but my home base for the moment is Cologne. Actually, not the city, but a small village fifteen minutes outside of town! It is surrounded by forests and lakes yet close enough to the city not to feel completely excluded. This location was chosen deliberately: the rent is much cheaper than in the city, I like to go for walks by the lake, and there is plenty of parking. But above all, I always play offense out here—in the city, you often only play defense. Everyone wants something from you, so they invite you to lunch, to coffee meetings, to drinks in the evening—your productivity often falls victim to the city. But my village location allows me to make the rules: I invite people to come to me if I want that, I have peace of mind, and I live according to my own schedule instead of the city's schedule, with its the rush hour and the crowds. I'm proactive and not reactive—a productivity strategy that allows me to do a lot more and be much more relaxed.

Find a location that positions you on offense, not on defense—then you'll score!

WHY ARE WE DOING THIS?

WHAT ARE WE THANKFUL FOR?

WHAT MAKES US STRONG?

HOW CAN WE PREVENT THAT?

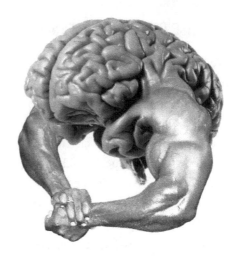

8. THE CREATIVE BRAIN AND YOUR BICEPS

The brain, like a muscle, is trainable. I like fitness. I go to the gym, pay attention to my diet, own expensive workout equipment, follow good exercise routines, and take food supplements. I have really made fitness a part of my way of life. Why? It provides a good balance. I start the day off right with a good workout and a healthy breakfast, both which cause the "I feel really good" neurotransmitters—like endorphin, dopamine, and serotonin—to get released into the body. It also results in a good physique—a nice side effect.

The killer: you can do exactly the same thing with your brain! Proof? The ability to orient oneself is located in the prefrontal cortex, which covers the frontal lobe of the brain. London taxi drivers have to deal with a super complex road network. Scientists have found that parts of their prefrontal cortex are much larger than those of other people. The continuous engagement with their work has led to actual brain growth—just like physical exercise leads to muscle development! It's like a ripped six-pack stomach, but in the head! The ability for the brain to change is called neuroplasticity. So, can we apply the lessons of the gym to developing our thinking, learning processes, and our continuing education? Can we consciously train our brains, especially the part responsible for creativity? Yes!

NO PAIN, NO GAIN!

Here's a mental equivalent of the bench press: try to write down three to ten ideas. The first few come easily, of course, but just like in training, the growth, the stimulus, the muscle building comes later, in the last repetitions. So, go where it hurts, where you think you can't push on, to the place where there seem to be no more ideas, no strength. Go beyond your boundaries, and you will grow!

By the way, all the other concepts from the gym can also be transferred to training the creative brain. Find a training partner who believes in you and can motivate you! Sports also teach you how to lose, emphasizing that a loss is simply feedback—it is not the end. The pain passes, the muscle heals—in the biceps, sure, but also in business and in life. Train regularly, note your progress, make a plan, eat well, don't skip training, educate yourself, read literature, and take breaks to recuperate. Never stop, be patient! Results don't happen overnight. When you try to integrate a whole new dimension into your life, you will only see the results in years, not days. Enjoy the journey, and don't fixate on your eventual arrival! Expose yourself to ideas, generate new ideas, and talk about ideas. Read, write, listen, and look. Keep going until it hurts and you'll eventually become really fit. No pain, no gain!

9. YOUR TEAM AND ITS MEMBERS

In the best teams, the members can get really loud with each other, not out of disrespect, but because each member is really prepared to defend their own opinions. "Yes-men" and pleasers can be quiet and uncomplicated, but they don't bring added value to the journey on the way to the best possible result. Our team gets rowdy again and again. Differences of opinion are quite normal, and every idea is immediately thought about, attacked, turned inside out, tested, and provocatively countered. Truly good ideas arise when the current status is challenged, when someone wants more, everyone critically questions your thoughts, and not everyone is satisfied with seemingly acceptable compromises. Always surround yourself with strong personalities and construct a team with a variety of skills and outlooks!

THE TYPICAL CANDIDATES FOR ALL-STAR TEAMS

THE TREND SCOUT

They travel a lot, browse, read everything they can get their hands on, talk to everyone, know everyone, have a good eye for things that work or they sense could soon work. An analytical hipster, a lateral thinker, not conventional but emotionally intelligent. A people connector with a black belt in small talk kung fu. They have lived abroad and sense the flow of trends. They're the first to spot the "next big thing," and they need a team to bring this observation to life. They say things like, "Infinitely scalable!"

THE CREATIVE

Horn-rimmed glasses, ultra-intelligent, draw freehand photo-realistic portraits, and understand art better than anyone else. Eloquent, a rhetorical sniper with an impressive specialist vocabulary from all sectors. They use artistic impressions from all over the world—which they've absorbed from museums, books, blogs, and studios—and mobilize them with perfection to create the face of a new idea. It's never only about what this face should look like, but—above all—it's about the "Why?" They do sharp-edged positioning and add almost imperceptible nuances which clearly set the product apart from anything familiar. They're freethinking artwork ninjas and can create gripping portraits from what previously were only ideas. They say things like, "Nice font!"

THE GENERAL

Brief, choppy sentences in both speaking and handwriting. Crystal clear announcements, brutal honesty. Primarily entrusted with the company's finances. They speak fluently about tax models, correct invoicing, and general accounting issues. The "Bad Cop" in every negotiation! They request missing bank statements and receipts and threaten consequences. They scrutinize each new idea through the lens of the finance department: What will it cost? Is it affordable? Realists, they use facts to bring every initial bout of euphoria—no matter how great—back down to the ground. Typically Excel professionals with an ultra-tidy desk and a color-coded, perfectly sorted document filing system. They say things like, "Yes, we're still in time for the 2% cash discount!"

THE WORK HORSE

The idea is on board—it already has a face and is financed, now such people arrive! Fit, strong, a leader and a go-getter. Fast, unerring, a game-maker and motivator. Organized and sympathetic, they represent the front line. They've got entire teams under them and bring the idea out onto the streets. Their plate is always too full because they're bombarded by everyone else, meaning they must control the flood of requests in order to be able to implement them. Like master bricklayers on the construction site, they erect one load-bearing wall after another. They dirty their hands, and move around. They're always there; everyone knows them and like them. They say things like, "Wow, I'm completely worn out!"

MARKETING MAVERICK

They have the "Four Ps" tattooed on their forearm (product, price, place, promotion). A cool nerd with a smart dressing style. They understand behavior patterns, anticipate the customer's perspective, juggle target group jargon with accuracy, and live on social media—both the backend and frontend. They attend seminars and understand the importance of A/B tests, research, and reach. They are not interested in sales, but in conversions and CPOs (Cost per Order). They don't argue with emotions, but with CTRs (Click-Through Rates), and drum together a following of loyal fans both online and offline who can really get the ball rolling. They say things like, "Call to action!"

YOU SHOULD REMAIN KEENLY AWARE OF THE FOLLOWING TYPES

THE SHARK

Tall, mostly good-looking, eloquent, opinionated. Be careful! They are always looking out for themselves—loners who are not afraid to take advantage of the group. The Shark is selfish, narcissistic, often treacherous, and stingy. Possible ways to cooperate: clear contracts, open discussions, clear communication, but in *no* case shareholding. It's like in scuba diving: Keep an eye on the Shark, don't panic, and show no fear. Keep this animal well fed, and the Shark is wonderful to look at, being capable of incredible performance. They often say things like, "I see it differently!"

EVERYBODY'S DARLING

A very nice person, but unfortunately a bit colorless. Always busy trying to please everyone, but unfortunately never able to follow through on anything. The following quote from Confucius perfectly describes the dilemma of Everybody's Darling: "If you hunt two rabbits, you won't catch one!" Their true nature usually only manifests after a long collaboration because in the beginning their weakness—disguised as niceness—remains under the radar. Since Everybody's Darling means well, it's only fair to help them by making it clear that their actual opinion is needed, even if it hurts them to share it. They often say things like, "Hmm, both are correct."

THE PESSIMIST

"Everything is difficult"—that's their motto. When things get really hard, their negativity can discourage teams from continuing or even getting started. There is always a fine line between true pragmatism and negative chatter. It's very important to spot their negative tendency as quickly as possible and either win over the Pessimist (which would also be a good exercise for sharpening your own arguments) or completely avoid working with them. They often say things like, "No, never!"

CHRIS NORMAL

The Problem: there are lots like them, and they don't mean any harm. But Chris Normal is so normal that all the key things you're into—your visions, your dreams, your plans—are just one size too large for them. They have never gotten out of their hometown, have never thought about seven-digit amounts of money, and prefer to be occupied and bound by instructions rather than by being free-spirited and visionary. It's an inspiring challenge for the leader to try to provide them with motivating visions that can help them grow beyond themselves. But often their attitude can't be helped—they're just "normal." Not necessarily a problem for them, but they are not valuable to your team! If you can't dream, you can't bring a dream into realization. They often say things like, "Really? That actually exists?"

EVERY TEAM HAS A COACH —FIND A MENTOR!

Before we get into the individual mentor types, here's a quick tip for finding them: *add value to your pitch.* An email like the following never works, "Hey, I think you're great! It would be awesome if we could go out for something to eat, and I could ask you some questions!" The key is adding relevant info. Find a person who knows everything you need to learn to get to where you want to go—for example, to where your potential mentor is right now. This is where diligence is required—it's a good investment: Read everything there is to read about this person, study their appearance (online/offline), watch videos, understand their strategies, approaches, goals, and positioning. Identify a part of his/her operation that can be optimized, and one that you can help optimize, thus saving your desired mentor time and energy.

THEN WRITE AN EMAIL LIKE THE FOLLOWING:

I'm sure you don't have much time, so I'll make this short: I looked at your videos online and thought they could be optimized. I'm a video editor. I've attached some of my current projects. I would like to edit and optimize your videos for you—free of charge—so that you can focus your scarce time on more important things. Like a delicious dinner on me because I have some questions to ask you about entrepreneurship. Does that trade make sense? (I read that you like sushi, and I know the best sushi restaurant in town.) Thank you in advance!

This kind of email is extremely effective, and it's difficult to refuse because the offered value is so strong. Do your homework and offer real value. What kind of email would you like to receive? Think in reverse!

THE FOLLOWING TYPES OF MENTORS TYPICALLY LIKE TO BE IN ON THINGS AT THE START

THE VETERAN

They've had enough. The Veteran has sold three companies, is a consultant for three more, is on the board of the Chamber of Commerce, is politically active, a great parent, is on the golf course every week, and is a real business veteran. Find this person and imitate them because they can really help you get ahead! Pay attention to their language and vocabulary, behavior, connections, experiences, mindset, values, and viewpoints. They have made countless mistakes from which you can learn, and that you can avoid making yourself. Because they started out like you, they're happy to share their knowledge. Emotions have become more important than money to the Veteran, and so sharing their knowledge and helping others triggers some of the best emotions they can get. Find them at receptions or at meet-ups (look for the person who knows everyone and who everyone knows), seminars (including the speakers or VIP guests), the golf course (or at tennis), in St. Moritz, in the south of France, at Burning Man, or in Palm Beach, Florida. The Veteran often says things like, "Splendid!"

THE YOUNG ELDER

The Young Elder is past his/her peak and essentially finished, but they still want to have another go at it! With a casual leather jacket and sneakers, they don't quite speak the language of the young entrepreneur kids, but definitely want to fit in. The power of these startup kids is contagious, and should help the Young Elder into their second (business) spring. Very cool because everyone is all fired up! Monthly advisor meetings, unlimited consulting calls, pitch trainings, and contacts are exchanged in return for the mentor feeling needed and able to help and give back. It's a win-win situation. Enjoy! They often say things like, "Good stuff! And now we're going out for a drink, aren't we guys?"

QUICK TIPS FOR RECRUITING YOUR TEAM

In addition to the team member types described in detail above, the best teams tend to consist of two types of employees: leaders and managers. (More on that later.) You must have both in your team. The value systems and approaches of these two types are completely different; therefore, they must be recruited in different ways. You find these people in different places, they have different tastes and expectations, and your game plans with them are 100 percent different.

HOW TO RECRUIT MANAGERS

- Job postings in the usual forums and magazines. Managers read about other managers.

- Clear task descriptions

- Good salary

- Clear structure and communication channels

The job ad describes what the person will do for the company.

HOW TO RECRUIT LEADERS

- Put job postings in unusual places and keep an eye out for recommendations that consider unusual angles. Leaders read about yachts or kitesurfing, and hang out in ski huts, at startup conventions, or at custom designed festivals in lesser-known places like Tulum, Bali, or the Australian hinterland. A good place to find leaders? In the gym or at yoga class in the mornings during the week. This means they have no conventional job to report to. In other words, they lead their own life. Connect the dots!

- Shares are always more important than salary.

- Keep the task description open, such as "Do whatever you think is necessary, as long as we reach our goals!"

The job ad describes what the company will do for the person.

These differences no longer apply when it comes to motivation. Once the positions have been filled with the right candidates, one all-encompassing motivational philosophy works, as long as the team spirit and corporate culture are strong (more on that later).

FIVE UNEXPECTED TRUTHS ABOUT MOTIVATION

MONEY DOESN'T MOTIVATE!

The greatest motivator is the promise of what you can become if you work hard enough, closely followed by being truly appreciated. The potential for people and companies to improve their view of themselves—along with serious praise—are the heavyweights of true intrinsic motivation.

PEOPLE WANT HIERARCHIES!

The common assumption that flat organizations motivate people is questionable. Hierarchical organization ensures clear communication channels. As long as employees are anchored in a functioning structure, they remain motivated. Confusion and uncertainty inhibit motivation, but hierarchies are supportive.

MOTIVATION THROUGH FUN
IS ONLY HALF RIGHT!

Yes, people want to have fun, and fun encourages motivation.
This doesn't mean that the workplace should be a playground.
Instead, people should derive enjoyment from doing good work.

THE NICE BOSS DOESN'T MOTIVATE!

The moment the boss places the interests of employees above
the interests of the company, he or she also puts them above
the interests of the customers and, thus, violates the basis and
raison d'être of the company.

SHARES IN THE COMPANY ARE NOT MOTIVATION!

I once thought that equity in my companies would motivate
my employees, but the opposite is the case. Most people don't
want to be entrepreneurs. Managers want to manage, without
risk. So let them do that, and motivate them instead with
big visions and real praise (see above). Shares simply do not
motivate them. Besides, underperforming employees would
never be satisfied with the offered shares. If too many shares
are distributed in the minor leagues, and only among the
midfielders, the only real result is a group of top-talent players
that are not motivated. Game over.

In his classic book, the business bible *Good to Great* (a must-read!),
Jim Collins talks about the "bus" as an important image for
visualizing a good team. Put the right people on the bus
and keep the wrong people off! Then, put the right
people in the right seats! This precaution ensures that
the bus arrives, even if no one knows where it's going. I
would go even further, and point out how important it
is for the bus to take the right route to pick up new people
(see recruitment), and that the bus' climate, legroom and
general comfort are optimal (keyword: motivation).

YOUR PERSONAL A-TEAM

Start your bus on its journey and go pick up your team—your
personal A-Team!

10. LESS IS MORE

"Necessity is the mother of invention." An old saying, but absolutely right! When your back is to the wall, you will find a way to get results. Inertia is always a danger to success, especially financial success. Don't get stuck questioning things when the result doesn't have to be perfect and there's nothing at stake.

With my team, the most influential, instructive, intensive, and above all, the fastest period of growth was when we were just starting out and had very few resources. Our original office was a Starbucks café (because of the free Internet). For nights on end, we filled and labeled the first NEONSPLASH–Paint-Party® bottles in my cellar.

We drove hundreds of thousands of kilometers, from party to party. We slept in our cars and lived in the office. We set up, ran, and dismantled the shows, taught ourselves everything, and reinvested every dollar in the company. Our fire was ablaze, not just because we were motivated, but also because there was no other way.

I know a lot of smart folks who get substantial financing before making their first profit, or even before proving market fit. A comfortable model, but in actuality a real pity because of the emotional experience they are denied. The teams that develop really good ideas are often the ones with hardly any resources, who are working out of tiny home offices or beat-up garages. There's a great metaphor for entrepreneurship: You jump from a skyscraper and you build an airplane on the way down. The attempt can end in disaster, of course, especially if you don't have a parachute. Since you jump free, and without a safety line, you may be really scared and give it all you've got! Make sure you see defeats as opportunities, and find the treasure in any situation, no matter how difficult they seem. The complexity of your challenge correlates with the genius of your results! And if you're truly burning to make something happen, everybody comes and wants to stand by the fire!

THE QUESTION OF MONEY: DOES "LESS IS MORE" ALSO APPLY?

"Money can't buy happiness," is another old saying. I need to briefly talk about it—especially in this chapter—because this statement has grabbed me repeatedly over the years, and made me think. My opinion: it's not true (at least, not completely).

This won't be a long discussion, but if that sentence has been haunting you, too, let's go through it together.

There is no doubt that, where you live, there's probably a correlation between happiness and money. In other parts of the world that have a shortage of water, food, or medicine, the people are often less happy and experience misfortune as a real physical threat. Hunger and pain lead to terrible suffering. But let's assume that the basics are available for all. If so, is a wealthy person inherently happier than someone with less purchasing power? The answer does not depend on the amount of money or purchasing power, but on the type of purchases. Think about it!

The perceived value of money is relative, and always connected with your emotions about what you can buy with it. For example, let's say you find $100 on the street. You would feel quite different if the same $100 were credited to your home utility bill. The objective value is the same, but the effect, the emotion, the *happiness* are totally different. The way money functions depends on what you do with it. People are happier when they spend money on others and not on themselves— this is scientifically proven. The happiness of making a gift is usually (especially in the long term) more important than the gift itself. Giving is always more empowering than getting.

Much unhappiness about money is related to having the wrong reasons for spending it. Walter Slezak once said, "Many people spend money they don't have to buy things they don't need in order to impress people they don't like." How true! The unhappiness stems from comparison and power struggles, taking place on the hamster wheel of a society motivated by envy. Those who always want a little more than everyone else will never be satisfied; their own happiness becomes a carrot on a stick, something that can never be achieved. The true beauty of giving is that a gift always gives more than anyone could have expected—and that's a win-win type of happiness.

And when you do buy something for yourself, make it something timeless—a purchase that you will always enjoy, that will never lose its charm, and that may provide more joy and happiness over time. Other purchases may involve things shared with friends: holidays, dinner, cinema, and theater, perhaps followed by great conversations that lead to real hugs, an honest laugh, or sincere tears. Give yourself and the people around you great memories, and the money you spend on them will really make you happy because it makes those moments possible.

Heads up: The opposite of happiness is not unhappiness, but boredom. And the greatest enemy of boredom is enthusiasm! Find something that honestly inspires and delights you and the greatest happiness will follow. How do you find that? What really inspires you? Finding out can sometimes be quite costly. So, I'm going to lay them out for free: Ask yourself what you would do if money suddenly didn't matter. If a billion dollars were in your checking account today, what would you do? What would you work on? What would be your goal? Your deepest inspirations are hidden in the answers to those questions! Take money out of the equation, and it all finally adds up!

2

MY 10 FAVORITE
IDEA-FINDING TOOLS

Okay, there are tools for this. Just like on every construction site in the world, there is a suitable tool for every problem. This is both good and important. Ever tried to hammer a nail into a wall with a screwdriver? It's not so easy! But when it comes to idea-finding processes, we often don't know beforehand whether we have to hammer a nail into the wall or whether there's even a wall in the first place. The idea creates the need. So, before you think about tools, you must first define the construction site. Like a pioneer, you make your way through unexplored terrain. Your only compass is your intuition.

Okay, you're not *totally* alone. Let me give you an orientation guide, a lighthouse that will at least show you in the right direction! I want to arm you with razor-sharp practical tools and theories for you to immediately produce ideas. These time-tested techniques for success will soon be yours. Just read on!

1. $100 PER DAY

It can be intimidating to face a potentially world-changing, million or billion-dollar idea. It's as if you were standing in front of Mount Everest and thinking about the strategy for the ascent. Important things to remember: every billion-dollar idea was once tiny, and every pro was once an amateur. The key: just deconstruct the big task into smaller tasks, and you'll automatically start climbing your own Mount Everest. Sure, there's a lot ahead of you, but at least you're on your way. The first step is always the hardest, but it places you in the top 1 percent of people who don't just fantasize and who really set out to make their ideas come true!

Your kickstart consideration is the following: How can I earn $100 today? Not $1,000, not $10,000, and certainly not $1,000,000,000. Start with $100! Remember, we just want to go for a walk—but without fear, without doubt, and with a clear goal. For now, it's still "only" about the first step. But as you think about how you can earn $100 today, you will find visions and ideas that will help you stay on course and pick up speed.

YOUR INTUITION IS YOUR COMPASS

Always write your ideas down immediately, otherwise you'll go in circles! Have you ever had an idea, or remembered something, and ten seconds later it's gone—as if it never existed? You're not alone. It's completely normal, but must be systematically prevented by writing down everything that comes to mind (using your mobile phone, a notepad, a napkin, or whatever else is lying around). Make it your goal to generate five ideas that could raise $100 today. Now it will get interesting! You have the foundation, now build on it!

How can you make your basic ideas bigger? For example, one of your ideas is to sell your old clothes on eBay. Okay, you can make $100 doing that today, agreed. But how can you make this idea really grow, and really become good? What if you sold more than just your clothes? What if you could potentially sell the clothes of every person in your circle of friends on eBay and get a percentage of the revenue for your service?

That's even better! And what if it's no longer just about your circle of friends, but about every person who wants to get rid of their clothes, but has no time, desire or expertise in eBay? What if you could systematize the individual steps required in the operation (photographing clothes, posting articles, pricing, managing reviews, etc.), in a way that could let you hand over the time-consuming operations to someone else? (This could be as simple as writing down all the steps. Or you could make a tutorial on your PC by using a screen recorder or using online collaboration tools, such as those available on Google Drive.)

QUICK TIP

Right from the start, think about how you can systematize and document the individual steps so you can eventually make yourself replaceable. This means your "next big idea" won't become a forty-hour week working IN the business, but rather ON the business.

The result: My friend, you just got a lot closer to the top of your Mount Everest, not because you're a magician, but because you simply got started, even though you started small. You've dodged your fears, created a foundation, and built on it. Facebook, one of the biggest and most influential business ideas of the last ten years, started as a network for a single university campus before it gradually picked up billions of users across the globe. Step-by-step, it's like "painting by numbers." Just get going on your path!

A very important note: Decide where your path might lead before you begin. Consider paths with infinite potential, without limitations. On which path can you help a billion people? Which path holds a promise of exponential growth?

AROUND THE WORLD IN 100 STEPS!

Before taking your first step, be aware of the power of exponential growth. If you walk 100 "normal" steps along your path, you are only 100 steps further. But if each step is exponential (for example: 1, 2, 4, 8, 16, 32, etc.), then after 100, you could have progressed over a billion steps further, the equivalent of walking around the world. Find a limitless path, think in terms of exponential progression, and then just put your first foot forward.

2. GO. STOP. BREATHE. GO!

Reflecting is perfecting. A sprint is great for covering as much distance as possible as quickly as possible, but how long can you sprint before you fall over from exhaustion? Be aware that you have finite energy, which you must leverage to the best of your ability. Step away from the task, and come back to it later. Take this time to gain insights and become aware of what is happening, and if you don't spot the details, ask someone else. It's a sure way to avoid "Could've, would've, should've." They say, "Hindsight is 20/20." Don't wait until it's too late and think, "If only I'd known that before!" Devote some time to reflection on a regular basis.

Let knowledge be consciously created, and then challenge it. Take a breath. Then, go again! Stop. Breathe. Go! Give it some gas, and then wait a little and check for interesting and unexpected results. This is where the true treasures are buried.

Every sprint gives birth to an insight. Go. Stop. Reflect. Evaluate. Recognize. Go again. Go at full speed! With that kind of varied pacing, you should be able to run your marathon.

BREATHE

When I say, "Take a breath!," I'm not telling you to breathe in and out. What I really mean is "Take a breath through your entire body!" Consider the practices of yoga, the ancient martial arts traditions from all parts of the world, the legendary Chinese and Indian theories about sexuality, spirituality, emotional relationships, the connection of body and mind, and the steel-hard power of the softness of the heart— all of them confirm that the secret lies in the breathing! Breathing brings life to the body. Very conscious, deep breathing immediately changes everything.

Try it out for yourself! Breathe slowly and deeply, through your nose, and deep into your torso. Imagine you want to blow your breath into an inflatable swimming ring to wear around your waist. Breathe deeply and calmly into your lower abdomen, into your back. Your breathing opens you to the world and to your gift, which you owe to the world.

Again and again I see people sitting or walking hunched over. Figuratively speaking, they have a knot in their being. This physical condition always carries over into the emotional. A hunched posture implies a hunched soul and a correspondingly "closed" life. Try to breathe when you're deeply hunched over. Yup, not happening. It's a contradiction. But straighten up, breathe deeply, and you will expand, feel strong, and be receptive to the others around you. People who connect are open; they open others through their aura.

Imagine you have a straight line that starts in the middle of your head, and runs down vertically through your body, through your tongue, neck, chest, and abdomen, down to your perineum (the point where your thighs meet). Along this line, you breathe through yourself and into the world. You inhale energy and life through your nose and then along this line deep down into your body. You don't breathe out this energy, but instead feel it travel up along this line, through your body, into your head. Visualize the oxygen, the life, dripping back down onto your body, like warm raindrops from your head.

Breathe consciously and you will know you are alive. Finally, you will be open to the insights that reveal themselves along your paths. Inhale these insights, inhale them to the top of your head, and really understand them in all their genius!

3. BRAINSTORMING, MIND MAPPING, ETC.

Children learn to speak through pictures, not words. Brainstorming and mind mapping are tools to force you to activate your right brain, the part responsible for creativity and imagination, so that you can visualize your thoughts in as unlimited a way as possible. They help you redefine connections, as well as understand conventional things in a completely new way.

For example, ask yourself "What can you do with a shoelace?" This question deliberately challenges your conventional and pre-programmed ways of thinking, to allow you to break through and engage completely new thought processes.

Here are the important factors for successful brainstorming:

YOUR PHYSICAL ENVIRONMENT

Where will your brainstorming session take place? Who will be there, listening and evaluating you, and how will they affect the session? Make sure your team is carefully selected, and establish clear rules for the brainstorming process. How much time will you allow for collecting ideas and connections, and when will they start to be systematically evaluated and attacked? Will there be a neutral mediator? After everyone has had their say, who will decide, regardless of the emotions of the group, whether an idea has merit?

YOUR EMOTIONAL ENVIRONMENT

Create an environment where you feel safe, strong, and empowered. It's not only about what you can see or touch, but about everything you sense and feel. Music, for example, always bypasses your intellect and reaches the deeper emotional realms of your being. So, provide your brainstorming session with background music, but make sure that it is suited to the task. For instance, your music selection can suggest calmness and relaxation, or power and speed.

Use headphones or a sound system with a lot of bass so you can feel the music in your body.

What is the room temperature? Is there food and drink? If so, what and when? Heavy and starchy food makes you lazy. Fruit, nuts, and water are absolutely beneficial but can be distracting if they are available at the wrong time.

Tips and ingredients for your perfect brainstorming session:

LIST OF MATERIALS
- Whiteboard (or flip chart) and markers
- Blank white paper (letter, legal, tabloid)
- Writing utensils (pencils with erasers / colored pencils / markers)
- Post-its
- Scotch tape

FOOD/BEVERAGE

- Water
- Fruit
- Trail mix

LOCATION

Table where everyone can sit and see each other (ideally round). If possible, at an unfamiliar location, or at least outside the customary workspace, and with minimal disturbance. (Avoid cafés and restaurants.)

PROCEDURE:

This is one of many possible procedures. Although I recommend the procedure below, there are certainly many other good possibilities. Try a few different ones and pick what works best for you and your team. In any case, I suggest that you retain the basic elements; they are tried, tested, and resilient.

- It's best to have a moderator—or even a mediator if required—who will be responsible for the relaxed flow of the session. This person does not lead but serves as a neutral guide. If they develop ideas themselves, they should quietly write them down.

- Provide three blocks of five minutes each during which ideas are openly collected, written down, and brainstormed. More time does not produce better results. People who think they need more time will subconsciously make the task more complicated and put themselves in a weak starting position.

- Each five-minute block has a defined goal, followed by a five-minute break. Music plays both during the active blocks and during breaks, but not the same type. During the breaks, everyone should get up and move around to try to switch their mental modes.

- During each block, the results (pages, drawings, mind maps) should be shared, so that people don't just continue to work on their own ideas.

- At the end of the idea-gathering period, the moderator should simply present the results without commentary.

- Immediately following is another five-minute block that people can use as they wish. They can write down ideas, think about them, or just get up and move around.

- Now comes the period for open discussion. We look for ideas and insights together and discuss whatever we've worked out. (Important: music continues to run quietly in the background.) The moderator leads the conversation with the goal of identifying one to three really good concepts for further discussion and development.

Once this goal is reached, the brainstorming session can end and the ideas are left to incubate for at least one night. After making any final changes or additions, the last step is, above all, to establish a clear action plan for implementing the ideas.

BASIC REMINDERS

- At least three people should be at the table. (A dinner duo is problematic, because two opinions tend to meet head-on. With three perspectives, it becomes interesting.)

- Between blocks, break up the group, move people around, and reconfigure. Doing so will stimulate fresh ideas.

- A maximum of ten people should be at the table in order to improve productivity and avoid confusion. If there are more people, simply divide them into smaller groups, separate them spatially, and combine their output later.

- Schedule a fixed time period: Brainstorming works only when everyone is fresh and sharp. No more than ninety minutes at a time!

- Good vibes: positive mood, no pressure, no fear. Encourage all input, and collect everything. There are no bad ideas here.

4. DIVERGENT VS. CONVERGENT THINKING

Before you start thinking about your next idea, clarify what kind of thought path you want to use to get to your goal. It's like deciding between a trip by car or train: in both cases you arrive at the same point, but the way you get there is different. The basic question is, "Divergent or convergent thinking?"

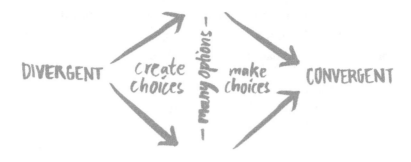

DIVERGENT

Imagine that you are shooting into the forest with a scattered firing pattern: you will surely hit something, but it's unclear what it could be. In a divergent thinking process, a person or a team produces as many different results as possible for later evaluation. In the second step, you can spot any intersections or matches. Like a person who fills out five lottery tickets, all of the scenarios are controlled by one entity. The potential for success results statistically from the large number of attempts.

CONVERGENT

In the forest, there's a hidden target, and five hunters are trying to hit it from different positions. With convergent thinking, the desired result is predefined and its production is outsourced to different people. The aim of the team is to move as deliberately as possible in the direction of the goal. Using different approaches is done in the hope that simultaneous effort and collective intelligence will hasten the goal.

5. FIVE PERSPECTIVES

There it is—a completely new idea! The catch: Is it for you or for your team to see it through to the end? But what if the people who designed and evaluated this idea (especially if it was just you) disregarded crucial perspectives? What if something really important wasn't considered, something that potentially could change the outcome?

It's time for a role-playing game. (I will describe the roles shortly.) All the strategically relevant perspectives must now be considered. You must encourage your role-players to give the performance of their lives because the quality of your results depends on it. You need five contradicting perspectives, played by volunteer actors who must be really "over the top" in playing their roles. Only through this exaggeration of emotions and opinions will you be able to arrive at the important insights that are the goal of this role-playing exercise.

THE OPTIMIST

What does the Optimist think about the idea? Of course, they find it *wonderful*, but why? Which opportunities do they see? How do they talk about the quality of this idea? All these answers must be considered even though they seem to live in a mental world where everything works and there is no resistance. Let the Optimist really step on the gas because it is their naïve daydreams that often help us look outside of the box.

THE PESSIMIST

To the Pessimist nothing works, but it's important to let the Pessimist describe what he or she thinks the problems are. They tend to spit on every little problem. They want to attack things that, at first sight, don't seem to be obstacles at all. Indeed, they even want to allow obstacles to arise. Their pessimism creates a gauntlet that the idea must now be run through. Where does the idea get stuck? Where do bottlenecks arise? What anticipated problems can be easily overcome, and which are truly and vitally problematic? The idea virtually receives a "baptism of fire." The more scathing the Pessimist's critique, the stronger the idea becomes.

THE REALIST

It's neither too good nor too bad; the Realist sees all the facts. Cool and calculating, they use sharp questions and put the idea's logic, viability, and potential to the test. It's all about hard data. Production costs, opportunity costs, potential revenue, time, strengths, weaknesses, and competition. If there are any leaks, they'll try to find and critique them. Like a shrewd detective, the Realist sets out in search of the truth.

THE MAD (WO)MAN

They must completely blow the idea out of its box. With endless imagination and pure openness, the Mad (wo)man sends the idea on a ride in the back of a train of confused combinations, completely new elements, and stark contrasts. They build, saw, connect, explode, scale up and down, and work like a child with modeling clay—with irrepressible joy and a clear lack of structure—producing a result that they themselves do not yet recognize. Their task is to find hidden, seemingly invisible, intangible ideas, and to combine them with the fundamentals. Have you ever encountered ideas that were so absurd that they could be considered brilliant? Genius and madness are close to each other, so let the Mad (wo)man embark on his/her journey, and have a pen and notepad ready.

THE WINNER

They speak from experience. They are no longer hungry and feel no pressure. Pressure, whether financial or social, blocks the right hemisphere of the brain, the one responsible for our imagination, visions, and emotions. The right hemisphere operates millions of times faster than the left, which controls our logic and rationality. Since the Winner is "done," they don't need the idea. Their task is to defiantly smile at you, and your task is to watch for moment they get excited, and note their reasons. The Winner looks for and recognizes the million-dollar opportunity. They're cold, uninterested, have no stress, and act level-headed. Their left brain lets the right brain incubate the idea in peace because there's nothing to worry about. And because they are calm, they subconsciously associate, check, and conduct hundreds of thousands of thought processes without knowing they are doing it. Their objectivity is extremely powerful because they don't *have* to win (not anymore).

6. SLEEP WELL!

During sleep, subconscious mechanisms and thought processes take place that we do not perceive. These can be incredibly valuable when we understand how to leverage them. Before falling asleep, ask yourself a question that addresses your task because you have the potential to generate really good ideas in your sleep! Believe in yourself, sleep on a question for one night, and—without any conscious effort—a great idea may emerge.

"BUSY-NESS" IS DANGEROUS

Sleep is much more important than you think. Modern company life has a "busyness" that is dangerous. It is scientifically proven that, after about six hours of work in the office on five to six hours of sleep, the human body is as "shot" as it is after six beers. How safe would you feel if the pilot of your next flight, or the dentist with a drill in your mouth, were in this condition? And yet we want to wrest more and more time away from the night to add to the day, without realizing that this very investment in a more "efficient" future is short-term and counterproductive. In the long run, sleeping less to work more completely destroys our creativity, health, effectiveness, and general well-being.

Here's a scenario that takes place every day in offices around the world. Employees come through the door and into the office. The boss asks, "Hi! How's it going?" The employee answers, "Good, thanks. Very busy!" They say that because they think their boss expects this answer. The boss, unfortunately, approves of this attitude, and does not notice how the employee is poorly managing time and resources. The boss is satisfied with "I'm fine, thank you!" What boss wants an employee who is simply "busy"? How productive is your work, really, when you're "busy"? And yet, "busy" seems to be the new "good." Why? Because then the boss might say, "Ah, you're fine, so you must not be busy. Here's more work for you!"

Tech companies in Silicon Valley, in particular, have recognized this nonsense, and include up to 20 percent "free time" in the daily schedules of their creative teams—time to take walks, have good conversations, sleep, eat well, find inspiration, listen to music, reflect, and establish personal connections.

Don't be busy being busy. Instead, give your creativity and your body enough sleep and freedom to really open up optimally, allowing yourself the energy to be able to solve world-class "thinking" tasks—not because you have to, but because you can! Sleep deeply, write down your thoughts, your dreams—get lost in them! What objects can you remember from your dreams, what were the emotions, who was there and what did they do? During the shower, the walk, or the short break, try to remember what your subconscious worked on and processed during the previous night. Tap into the infinite and inexplicable abilities of your subconscious. Sleep well, rest, relax, recharge. Again, don't just be busy being busy!

7. WRITE IT DOWN

How many times has an idea shot into your head—apparently out of nowhere—and was gone again, just as fast as it came? It's a common problem, and often the reason why grandiose killer ideas are never brought to life. To solve this, make sure you have a medium always at hand so that you can immediately capture your situational genius! You need a system that ensures that everything great that happens to fly by gets snagged and captured.

When I'm on the road, I store everything in my smartphone. I use both notes and my calendar so I can control exactly when I'm reminded of the idea. I often program these reminders so that the idea will be displayed again at a time when I know I will be in the office or sitting with my team, in which case I can throw the idea to the group to see how it plays—the more eyes and ears, the better. Pen and paper come in handy, too, because one internalizes the idea via the act of "writing it down"—tattooing it on the brain, so to speak. Your subconscious now knows that you are actually listening and will continue to suggest ideas to you. Alert your subconscious; don't be like a bad friend who lets everything pass by unmentioned.

You will design your own archive of ideas, thoughts, pictures, and strategies. You can use this archive at any time, to browse, think further, connect, and allow yourself to be inspired. So write down everything that has not already been nailed down—every word has immeasurable potential value!

8. FIFTY IDEAS / MANY MORE COMBINATIONS

Good ideas are often the result of traditional variables that are recombined into really new killer formulas:

COLOR + MUSIC + SHOW = (NEONSPLASH – PAINT-PARTY®)

The art lies in the momentum, in the moment, and in fearlessness.

MY TIP

Quickly come up with fifty basic ideas! Don't initially focus on quality. These fifty "blanks" are then combined with each other. The potential combinations are gigantic. But how else are you going to come up with the really absurd ideas that actually work: Ice cream with whipped cream, shoes that light up (we've all had them, ha ha), a camera in your telephone? Innovation is combination. Give in to the rhythm, and produce these ideas *en masse*, against every convention and without being shy! The evaluation comes at the very end, after all the combinations have been laid out. Only then can you sift, discover, think, grasp. The hardest step is usually the first. Just get started and make it happen! You will be amazed at how much material you can produce.

INNOVATION IS COMBINATION!

9. MATTHEW'S CREATIVITY COCKTAIL TECHNIQUE

The role of the Creativity Cocktail technique is to unlock creative bandwidth and reveal an idea's untapped potential. The technique takes seemingly colorless basic ideas and shakes them up, checks them from all angles, pulls, stirs, pushes and changes them until something very special emerges. With systematized chaos, the Creativity Cocktail technique grabs even the most lackluster ideas and straps them onto a rocket of possibility and madness. Let's shake and stir things up, using NEONSPLASH – Paint-Party® as an example.

COMBINATIONS

What could we combine with NEONSPLASH – Paint-Party® to make the experience even more interesting? We turned our focus on the film industry. We combined the paint-party concept with a special cinematic experience and produced a complete European tour in 3D—

image effects, 3D glasses, and so on. This unconventional combination of two genres created a noticeably sharpened USP (Unique Selling Proposition). The subtitle ("The 3D Experience") has enabled us to restage a familiar concept in a cost-efficient and media-effective way. Always combine your idea with new variables and continue to create new incentives!

ALTERNATIVES

Is there an alternative? Would it be possible to exchange key components and thereby invent really exciting new concepts? What if the dress code at a NEONSPLASH – Paint-Party® was no longer white but black? Could we change the type of music, appeal to a completely new target group, and create an entirely new idea by deliberately changing one or two elements? Yes. Among our offerings, we have a Hardcore-Paint-Party® Concept, which uses much heavier techno and hardstyle music, along with a black dress code and darker colors. Creating a well-chosen alternative to a single element of your idea is often enough to open up a whole new market.

ZOOM IN, ZOOM OUT

Operational blindness is a widespread disease among entrepreneurs. You're so busy every day with your idea that you can see the tress, but not the forest. Determining the bestselling points becomes more difficult; everything is blurred. So take a few moments to look at your idea, your business, through the lens of an imaginary camera, and just change the zoom! Zoom far out to notice whatever else is happening around your idea, what spin-offs might be available, what else the market has to offer, what works and what doesn't, as well as why! How does your idea work in the larger context? The further you zoom out, the more interesting these insights become. And if you discover something on the periphery of your idea, then point in that direction, zoom in, and magnify the new prospect. Consider what might be possible there and inspect every opportunity. Then zoom back out and look at the long shot again.

With NEONSPLASH – Paint-Party®, this zooming technique helped us launch our international expansion. We implemented the first event in Cologne, experienced very rapid growth, and dominated the market. For many, this would have been a dream scenario, and the end of a beautiful local success story. But what happens when you zoom out?

Other big cities suddenly come into view and you identify new opportunities. Still further out, you start to notice whole new countries. The right perspective produces true opportunity—change it often!

APPROPRIATION

Does a confetti cannon always have to shoot confetti? What happens if you envision an alternative purpose for a conventional device that no one else has considered before? When we first tried to convince a mechanic to help us build fully-functional Paint-Party® paint guns by re-purposing confetti cannons or pond pumps, he was extremely confused and skeptical. For a long time, we appropriated, rebuilt, reconsidered, and realigned established equipment until our understanding was so optimized that a Dutch team of special effects manufacturers was able to rebuild the basic design and create the type of paint guns we needed.

If your idea does not yet exist, then use existing materials until others can understand and implement your vision—even if there has never been anything like it before!

SUPPORT

What happens to the most talented player on a soccer team or the smartest child in the class? Their talent is recognized, promoted, and supported. This helps them reach their potential and ensures their maximum performance. It's the same with the really strong elements of your idea: What works really well? Who is the truly talented player on your team? This is exactly where you should focus your attention because this is where you leverage the biggest 80/20 effect. (According to the Pareto principle, 20 percent of your inputs produce up to 80 percent of your results.) Identify these success drivers and support them!

When we realized the high demand for paint at NEONSPLASH – Paint-Party® (not just shot off the stage, but also sold at the show), we created sophisticated sales mechanisms that more than doubled our sales. We had sales booths adapted for the large crowds, a cashless token system to minimize transaction time and to prevent theft by our own staff, and we had visual effects that encouraged guests to purchase the paint. With these additional features, sales exploded and the guests' experience significantly improved. Find out precisely the parts of your idea that work really well and give them support!

ELIMINATION

Less is more. As I'm writing this book and rereading what I've written, I delete passages again and again. For me, it's about producing really dense content so I don't waste your precious time. It's the same with really good ideas. The question isn't "What can I add?" but "What can I leave out, in order to provide better density, clarity, and simplicity?" It's not the "Yes" things that set the necessary focus on the essentials, and move us forward, but all the things to which we say have to say "No."

When Steve Jobs worked at PIXAR, he learned what focus really means. They all worked together for three years on a single project, without exception, and without distraction.

The project was called Toy Story, one of the most successful animated films of all time. Returning to Apple with this knowledge, he eliminated entire product and business lines, and focused only on carefully selected segments: PCs, MP3s, laptops, and later on mobile phones and tablets. The result is one of the most successful companies in the world.

FIND YOUR "TOY STORY"!

Concentrate on the essentials, reduce your idea down to the basics, say "No" more often than "Yes," and find out what your "TOY STORY" is.

ADJUSTMENT

Have you ever gotten lost driving a car? No problem, it happens to everyone! The solution: we simply adjust our route to reach the goal. It's the same with really good ideas. Your idea is moving along and everything seems fine, and then suddenly you realize that you're no longer on course. Operational blindness. One short, unfocused moment and you miss the exit. Adjusting your route is perfectly normal because there's no automatic navigational device for your entrepreneurial adventures. Don't be shy about going full throttle in the wrong direction. As long as you have the wits to adjust your path, to reorient yourself, to reflect, to change your idea, and to realign yourself toward the ideal course, then the market will show you the way. Be sensitive to the right path!

10. EXPOSE YOURSELF TO NEW THINGS!

When I was a fourteen- or fifteen-year-old troublemaker, my mother told me "Matteo (my mom is Italian, and Matteo is the loving Italian version of Matthew), broaden your horizon. That's the most important thing!" As a young dude, I never really understood what she meant, but I have always followed her advice. I lived and studied abroad for a long time. (Disclaimer for all those who now think, "Sure, if my parents had the money, I'd do the same!"—but this was mostly via scholarships.) I've gotten to know many different people from all over the world, tried countless things I couldn't do or didn't know enough about, and constantly was involved in projects for which I was hardly qualified or not qualified at all. I read a lot, asked a lot of questions, talked a lot, made a lot of mistakes, and was (and still am) curious and inquisitive.

"YOU ARE THE AVERAGE OF THE FIVE PEOPLE YOU SPEND THE MOST TIME WITH!"

—JIM ROHN

Exposing yourself to new, unknown things is always the fastest way to new ideas. When you break away from the norm and old processes, the fresh wind and the slight insecurity will keep you on your toes and you'll stay "sharp." You know what's really impressive (and this is a relatively new understanding for me from the last ten or fifteen years)? You come to realize that you actually hold the world and all its influences in your hands, always on call, no matter where you are. Take advantage of it! I have subscribed to twelve different business podcasts, produce my own weekly podcast called "Smart Entrepreneur Radio," and receive about twenty entrepreneur blogs and online magazines in a continuous feed. I also follow world-class entrepreneurs and thinkers like Mark Cuban or Tony Robbins on their social network so I can partake of their thoughts and visions again and again. One of the most successful motivational trainers of all time, Jim Rohn, said "You are the average of the five people you spend the most time with!" So, use modern technology and associate (at least digitally) with the most exciting and inspiring thinkers of all time!

Exposing oneself to new things also means being fearless. Always get yourself into situations that overtax you: don't be afraid of being the dumbest at the table, the weakest in the gym, the most inexperienced in the group, and absorb anything new that gets between your fingers! You won't find your best ideas, food for thought, stimuli, and inspiration where you are looking for them. Instead, you'll find them where you dare to go—outside all the situations you already know. Expose yourself to new things, and your best ideas will arise all by themselves. Just watch!

3

MY FAVORITE 10
IDEA-EVALUATION
TOOLS

___

Whatever isn't measured will also not be improved. Therefore, create ideas, and then step back again and again and use the following approaches to examine your results! It's not about right or wrong, good or bad, yes or no. Get accustomed to constructive reflection. Evaluating is as important as developing. Detach your emotions from your project and honestly reflect on your progress! Forget worrying about time or money spent. In one minute of honesty, you'll realize that the only way out of a hole is to stop digging.

I want to show you a new way to look at things—a perspective that will provide endless insights. By the end of this chapter, you will be able to do the following in order to effectively and efficiently make decisions about any idea:

- PURSUE,
- ADJUST, OR
- THROW OUT

1. CRITICS

The person who least likes your service, your product, or your idea is the most important person you need to consult with in order to really move forward. Yae-sayers, proponents, and optimists are important and nice to have, true. Yet, if you really want to make big jumps forward, get someone who is very hard to impress and who criticizes in detail (but objectively and purposefully). From the critic, you will hear what didn't work, what was really bad, or what was good but could be even better. Take it all in, but don't take it personally! Don't ask, "What was good?" but instead ask specifically, "What was bad?" Of course, critical feedback is endurable only in doses, but this type of feedback is worth its weight in gold. Find your "Captain of Critique," and use him or her! On our team, it's Florian—friend, co-founder, creative director, and "Mr. Hard-to-Impress." When everyone is already loving it, he's still unimpressed. His own artistic designs are always only acceptable to him in their fifth or sixth version. When I ask him for feedback,

I know that nothing really euphoric will come back, but his critique is where the treasure is buried. We love and respect each other like brothers, especially when it comes to important feedback. Here, you don't want to please. You want to improve.

The helping hand doesn't just applaud—it shows the way, helps you up, admonishes you, and never lets you go! Find really good critics, and your ideas will explode!

2. POTENTIAL CUSTOMERS

Put yourself in the shoes of your potential customers. Really go into detail. What do they look like, where do they go shopping, how old are they, what moves them, what are their problems, what are they afraid of, and what do they really need? Marketing, idea development, and strategies are always much more effective if you start with the customer. If you starts with the product, you have to push the product on the customer (which costs time and money, and isn't particularly interesting). If, on the other hand, you start with the customer, you don't have to force anything on them. On the contrary, the customer will automatically find your product attractive because you anticipated beforehand what they really need.

VIRALITY CANNOT BE FORCED!

When we started out with NEONSPLASH – Paint-Party®, the German party scene was completely asleep. The ten thousandth "Best of House and R&B" party? Nobody wanted that anymore. Our potential customers wanted more: a new experience, something they could tell their friends about, something they would gladly post on their social networks.

The keyword here is "gladly." Some marketers try again and again to force virality. But if someone "gladly" shares something simply because it's so good and cool and solves a problem, that means it's really interesting. Put yourself in the shoes of your potential customer, find out what they need, and give it to them—the rest happens all by itself.

3. SYSTEMS VS. HUMANS

Good ideas are replicable, systematical, transferable, and scalable. Create ideas based on systems, not on people!

Do you know about the really good restaurant in your town, with the nice owner, Luigi, who knows your name, who's always there, and who really is the soul of the restaurant? Of course! I know him, too. Every town has this restaurant, and every restaurant has this guy.

Luigi's problem is that he can only be in one restaurant at a time. Do you understand what I'm saying? He's an impeccable host, his restaurant is awesome, the menu is perfectly laid out, lots of nice ideas have been neatly implemented, but he cannot reproduce his operation—the numbers and math won't let him do that.

Here's a small calculation example. (I hate math, but love its honesty—I promise this will be easy.) We will now compare the figures of an unscalable activity like Luigi's (by the way, every service provider, employee, or anyone who exchanges time for money is also unscalable) with the mathematics of a scalable "next big thing." Revenue always depends on two variables: units and price (for the moment, we'll disregard costs). If you trade time for money like Luigi, your units are the hours you can work: about eight hours a day and the price is your hourly wage.

UNITS PRICE = REVENUE

To make it easy let's look at a standard salary: With 8 units (= hours) per day (25 working days per month), and an hourly wage of $15.00, this produces $120 per day, or $3,000 per month. Let's manipulate the variables that produce this result. Work more hours? If he works 24 hours—that's what Luigi does for three days straight before the pizza oven shuts down forever! But let's consider a more realistic 10 hours per day. And a higher hourly wage? All right, let's go crazy! Luigi now collects the hourly wage of a lawyer or surgeon: $300 per hour would be worth it—if his pizza saves lives and marriages! Our new revenue:

10 HOURS $300 = $3,000/DAY

The amount looks wonderful but the formula has built-in limitations. Nobody can work more than 24 hours in one day, and few people— we leave out special talents like celebrities and athletes—can achieve even a 100 percent salary increase. Usual salary increases are only 5-8 percent (if you can get them at all), and definitely don't happen every year. So, when it comes to hourly wages, we are always operating in a limited number range.

But big numbers don't like boundaries. Here is Luigi's best case, summarized:

UNITS PER DAY (HOURS): 10
PRICE: $300
REVENUE (UNITS X PRICE): $3,000

In your scalable "next big thing," using systems that don't require a Luigi, the variables can be manipulated differently, so that the whole basis of your mathematics changes.

Let's take software projects as an example, such as those from Oracle:

UNITS PER DAY (MEASURED BY THE SIZE OF THE MARKET): 100,000+
PRICE (PER ARTICLE): $80,000+
REVENUE (2014): ABOUT $8,000,000,000

Large numbers generate large results. Systems leverage large numbers. Your "next big thing" must not be limited by mathematics. So, don't exchange time for money!

What if your numbers are smaller than those for Oracle?

Don't be discouraged if your product doesn't allow for huge numbers per unit. There are stunningly impressive micro SaaS (software as a service) start-ups built by one person or small distributed teams that create high margin, recurring, predictable revenue, with low risk and location independence. They address a huge and growing market of Internet entrepreneurs looking for smart tools. If you are a solo entrepreneur, and 1000 people use your $19 per month SaaS product, you have undoubtedly created something amazing, despite the seemingly small numbers!

As long as the success of the pizza depends on Luigi's presence, he is a slave to his own machinery, making himself indispensable and paralyzing his opportunities for growth. Really resilient ideas are based on systems, not on people. It's not Mark Zuckerberg himself who connects billions of people worldwide on his Facebook social network; it's a system on which his idea-of-the-century is built.

Always ask yourself: "What happens if I'm sick for six weeks?" Will everything continue as usual? Create automatic mechanisms! With NEONSPLASH – Paint-Party® we were able to organize three shows at the same time. This is because, from the very beginning, we made the processes, the materials, the employees, and the expertise reproducible. Make yourself replaceable, systematize all processes, and transfer the risk and implementation to as many different bodies as possible. A person creates the idea and turns it into a system that can stand on its own feet and keep going—letting them invest their capital gains (money and time) into the development of ever new ideas and systems.

ROBUST IDEAS ARE BASED ON SYSTEMS, NOT ON PEOPLE.

4. HOW BIG IS THE PROBLEM THAT WILL BE SOLVED?

Apart from the idea itself, the problem that the idea can solve is a perfect starting point for asking questions about relevance: Who benefits from your solution? Who suffers from the problem you will solve? Is the problem really a problem? Is the idea a real solution? Or, is it just a relocation of the problem? A suitcase is a good idea that solves a problem, for sure. But let's ask about the exchange of values: Does the idea return more than it demands? The suitcase is, without a doubt, a good idea. Now let's add wheels to the suitcase (an "innovation" that was developed decades after the invention of the suitcase). Suddenly, due to its relevance to a related problem, the original suitcase idea takes on a completely new value—in retrospect, so simple, useful, and obvious that you have to ask yourself, "Why didn't I think of that?"

In the search for solutions to problems, it's crucial to be able to abstract. Don't just respond to symptoms, but trace each problem back, and discover the original mistakes. In his incredibly powerful book, *The Millionaire Fastlane*, MJ DeMarco provides a very fitting illustration that shows the difference between symptoms and the real problems: A leaking fuel tank is the symptom; refueling more often is the solution. The real problem, however, is the hole in the fuel tank. Solve problems; don't treat symptoms!

To assess the magnitude of a problem, it is helpful to measure it in different contexts. If you solve a small problem for a large number of people, the per capita value of your solution

QUICK TIP

It's always easier to grow out of a niche than to develop a new suitcase. Talk to your customers and solve their problems. Often, your customers will give you your next idea. Just listen well!

is small, but the number of fixes that are accomplished is large because many people have the same problem.

If you solve a big problem for a small number of people who attach great value to your solution or the problem, that market is also financially effective.

Condense the way you measure relevance into two dimensions: think 100 miles wide and 1-inch deep for ideas that everyone needs (such as the suitcase), or 1-inch wide and 100 miles deep for very specific, and therefore valuable solutions, such as unique software for real estate agents.

5. WHAT MAKES THE COMPETITION BETTER/WORSE?

The moment you are no longer the only one with an idea, your version will be directly compared to that of the competition. Like your potential customers, you must be able to objectively understand whether your idea has elements that are implemented better or worse than the competition. If someone else is doing things better, use this insight as a benchmark, and make it your goal to become at least ten times better than they are.

In his book *Zero to One,* PayPal founder and first Facebook investor, billionaire Peter Thiel, talks about the 10x Rule, which states that in order to really enjoy and justify a noticeable edge and relevance as a market leader, you should be at least ten times better than any other player on the market.

If the competitor is worse at implementing some of the elements, you should likewise identify these vulnerabilities, and directly address them. If your competitor is lagging in quality, then you should make your competitive advantage even more obvious by improving your current quality. Having a better understanding of where you stand in the brutal hierarchy of the market will help sharpen your strategy and determine your plan. When you know where you stand, you know exactly where you have to go!

6. THE 3D PHOTO: JOURNEY FIVE YEARS INTO THE FUTURE!

A quick evaluation of your idea is only a snapshot. Everything is clearly recognizable, but there's little depth. Imagine being able to dive into that photo and explore its past. A third dimension suddenly opens up and you can go back to the beginning of the idea—back to the very first step, your most important step ever—when your overwhelming motivation and will won the battle against your fears and ignorance.

But your future is even more important. So follow the timeline of your idea in the other direction, far ahead, into the future! Travel five years forward and take a good look: Where are you, and with whom? What has worked, and what hasn't? What did you concentrate on, and why? And what has it brought you? Who is still with you? How does it feel? How has your idea developed, who benefits from it, and what are its values? Are you happy, are you proud? Drink it all in, take a close look at everything, understand it in detail, and then bring it back into the present. Step out of your photo and take another look at where you are at that moment. Rejoice because the moment belongs to you alone, built on all the actions of the past, and full of potential and knowledge from the future. You've seen what it's going to look like, so set your course and go where you need to go. You are familiar with that place because you've been there before.

7. START AT 100!

There's a correlation between bad and good ideas. If you produce a lot of really bad ideas, you will also—statistically speaking—generate many really good ideas in proportion. Write down 100 ideas, but keep in mind that you only start to seriously evaluate ideas starting with idea number 101! Your brain, according to neuroscientific evidence, is naturally conditioned to save energy. It takes the shortest route—always. This route first leads you through familiar experiences and ways of thinking, as well as systems and connections that you already understand. Your first 5, 10, 100 ideas are easy routes, unexciting. They are safe. But from the 100th idea onward, it becomes interesting. (Don't shoot me down, my friend, if it starts at idea number 80 or at 120 for your best buddy.) The easy paths are no longer open, and you are forced to fight against ignorance, short-sightedness, lack of experience, and insecurity. But this is where the music plays. In these remote corners of your mind (conscious and unconscious), the great treasures lie buried. It's like a soccer player who becomes truly stoked during the stoppage time after ninety minutes of play. During that pause is when he suddenly notices how much he wants to win. He knows he must now use every fiber in his body and call up his reserves of strength and endurance, because now he knows he has to.

Statistically speaking, you rarely get a real hit in relation to all the attempts you try. Love every "No" because it brings the next "Yes" closer. *Ready, Fire, Aim* by Michael Masterson is one of the best books on systematically building your business in all its stages of growth—a must-have recommendation from me if you want to save a lot of money. In his book, Masterson talks about having a main product that generates "traffic" and lures people through the door so you can offer numerous secondary products. The main product—your best horse in the stable—must be really good, otherwise it won't get anyone through the door or in front of your other products. But you must create each of your products with the hope that it may become a winner, a real main product, the darling of the audience. Though this is statistically rarely possible, your demand for quality and innovation will raise the average quality of the entire product range, and your secondary products will also become really good because they are near-hit attempts at a main product. Now your rocket is in orbit. You've created a primary product that attracts people; your shelves are full of other strong products that generate real sales. Your customers have come through the door, and they trust you. Reward their trust with the highest quality! Raise standards, build each product with a winner in mind, push your limits, dive really deep, and discover the most beautiful pearls down there!

8. YOUR CREATIVE FRIEND

Every team, every circle of friends, every office, and every party always has someone who's the creative type. They stand out because they're different. They look deeper, see more, and think differently than the others. Show them your idea, and then just listen! The dimensions they dive into, the potentials they focus on, and the places where they think one step further are decisive building blocks for your foundation. Even though your business is ready to get moving, you still holding the foundation in your hand. Your idea can go even deeper, and your creative friend will show how. Leave your ego at your creative friend's door. You don't know everything, you're not "finished" and there is much, much more to create than you ever thought.

Your human resistance to change and to novelty may turn your creative friend completely inside out. But let go and watch them take your idea and run with it. Don't feel left behind, feel supported! As with your training partner in the gym, your creative friend helps you realize your potential powers and do the seemingly impossible. Let yourself be pushed—go with it. Your creative friend senses exactly where to go, so rely on him or her!

I keep hearing people say "I don't want to tell you anything. What if my idea gets stolen?" An important point and a justified fear. But—

and this "but" is important—this over-caution is also the reason why many really good ideas don't even make it out the door. How many times have you said to yourself, "I had that idea a while ago!" or "I could have thought of that, too." But you never did anything! Why? Maybe because you didn't venture into the open. A world-changing idea, trapped in the silent secrecy of your personal thoughts, or shared only with a small circle of friends, can have a hard time developing legs. So go out, talk about your idea and get feedback, develop your thoughts, and revise your plan accordingly.

IT ALL DEPENDS ON THE IMPLEMENTATION

Implementation is much more important than the idea itself. Long before Facebook, and during its early years, there were many other social networks. Some had a stronger financial background and a healthier stamina, as well as had teams that were more experienced and had better qualifications. But they didn't necessarily have the best implementation. With NEONSPLASH – Paint-Party®, we had—and still have—imitators, but it isn't enough to just copy the idea. Your uniqueness is what allows you talk to anyone about your idea without worrying that it might be taken away from you. What makes you special is the interplay of your creativity, your experiences, your concepts, and visions, along with your idea and your team (especially the ace up your jersey sleeve—that creative friend). Nobody may have expected it, but you're the winning team. Your moves will likely get stolen, but never your spirit, never your will, and never your friendships!

YOU NEED A STAR!

9. AUDITIONING FOR IDEAS

With so many television reality shows where people vie to become stars, you surely must know how it works. Apply this process to the evaluation of your ideas. An idea introduces itself—sometimes well, sometimes not so much, but always with the hope of making a difference. Now it's up to you to notice any potential talent. Can you spot the Star, even if it's incognito? As the casting agent, do you have the imagination to foresee potential—yet unwritten—success stories? As an agent, what are your own qualities? Are you hard, soft, nice, evil, honest, or restrained? Face your auditioning ideas as if they are young talent, who want nothing more than to be break into show business. You control the next round of auditions. Be rigorous and give a good amount of thought about which idea should advance and why. Your ideas must survive three rounds to reach the grand finale.

ROUND 1

Does this idea serve the basic requirements of a scalable business model? Looks nice, it can sing, it can dance: it passes! This is how you should see the first round of your idea casting. Is the foundation alright? Be tough, but fair. Gladly leave behind the wrong ideas. It's the things you say "No" to that are really important, not the things you say "Yes" to. Be choosy and farsighted. In this first round, all of the trash is sorted out. Ideas that just aren't made for the spotlight get canned. To those that are overrated, but are unfortunately neither sound nor tactical: *Sorry. Next, please!*

ROUND 2

Which of the remaining ideas have clear strengths, or dangerous weaknesses? How do they stand in relation to the market? You're facing a really solid group now. They can all at least do something. Look closely! Are there exceptional talents, real high-flyers, or clear weaknesses? Where do they stand in relation to each other? What's the potential of the weaker ones? What are the leaders' long-term strengths? After you understand the group, its range of qualities, and its outstanding individual potentials, you must analyze this group with regard to the market. Look beyond your casting couch. Which of them are standing on the big stages? Who is inspiring the fans? Whose posters are hanging in every room? Are there intersections, similarities, or clear guidelines dictated by the market? Who is currently competitive? Are there "gap fillers" in your group? Can you spot completely new starting points or daring combinations, and can you see a clear chance of success for one or another? Understand your talent pool as a microcosm, and then evaluate how the members of this short list might function under the spotlight of the Big Boys of the market—the ultimate stage.

ROUND 3

This top-level round is about putting it all into practice: up here, the air is thin and the quality is outstanding. All of these ideas are live grenades in this open field. The only question is, "Who takes off first and for how long?" It's not just the best, but also the fastest who wins the race for the hearts of the fans. A contestant with an adequate voice and execution might require an extended launch, for instance, another two years of artistic development to perfect their songwriting skills. *No, thank you.* What you need is a finished Star—polarizing, already noticeable in the run-up, different, outrageously talented, and groundbreakingly unique. Everything should be on point: the look and the voice, the dance moves, the style, the attitude, the personal story, the feelings, the *magic*. All this, coupled with charming modesty and priceless values, and suddenly this artist is an asset. They don't want much but give everything and get everyone. That's your Star. That's the "next big thing." Congratulations, this idea is the winner, it's the star!
Now shine its light on the world!

10. WHAT WOULD IT COST YOU TO QUIT?

Your idea is standing out there. You have taken the first step, and now you are hearing the professionals applaud from the VIP grandstand. Our society respects people who start something and loves the moment of the first step. We celebrate the first day of school, the first kiss and the engagement, the beginning of advanced studies, a new registration at the gym, the new year with all its good intentions. A clean slate and new beginnings are always a reason for joy. It's on its way! Super!

The logical consequence is that many people naturally manage to get started. Yet, the sad truth is that very few finish what they've begun. Not everyone graduates from high school with a diploma, few students go on to complete a degree, few marriages last forever, and the gym is already half-empty again in March. Why? Because the result is costly. You can estimate its value by the amount of resistance met on the way to the result. There is not an overabundance of heart surgeons because the study is strenuous and requires a lot of discipline, therefore the cost for their service is also high because the demand exceeds the supply. Not everyone is fit and muscular because it takes time and discipline. Not every marriage lasts forever because a functioning partnership requires real work.

DON'T QUIT TOO SOON!

A big problem is the timing: people always stop at the wrong time. They give up just before it gets interesting.

For example, the marathon runner doesn't stop after one mile while she still can hear the cheering from the starting area. No, she only stops only after reaching the finish line. The solution: Don't start anything you won't finish, and you'll save yourself time and attention. Don't waste opportunities and weaken your stamina by turning onto roads that have a no-outlet sign. In his book *The Dip*, Seth Godin dissects this problem in fantastic analytic detail. The later you quit, the more expensive it gets for you, the higher your deficit. But if you don't even start a project because you know that you won't finish, your account remains balanced. The greatest potential lies in the disproportionate reward you receive the moment you finish a project. Every meter of your marathon makes you the person who arrives at the finish and is absolutely essential, but the champagne shower waits until after you cross the finish line. Know that it will be difficult and that it will not immediately work out, but never forget that you either have to cross the finish line or get out before giving up gets expensive.

Let's evaluate your idea in terms of the cost of your potential exit: If your idea is like a jumbo jet, your idea should have wings, of course, but how long is the runway? How much thrust do you need, how much kerosene do you have to burn to make this thing take off? If your idea is like a pyramid, and you say "I'm building this pyramid all by myself," it will certainly take a few decades. In that case, your "runway" is extremely long, and the cost of demolition halfway through is enormous.

In the evaluation phase, you should already be focusing on the potential costs of your exit. When evaluating, you should not even start if these costs are too high, or if you could invest your budget more efficiently on another idea with a shorter runway. If you have carefully read the last nine strategies, then you know that my system for evaluating ideas works, but you have one more consideration to make. There are great but expensive ideas out there that you shouldn't even start if you can't afford to jump ship a few months in. Be an aircraft carrier, from whose short runway many jets take off daily! Throw a lot into the air and evaluate the path to the goal, not just the expected result.

4

10 TIPS FOR "SUCCESS THOUGHTS" THAT GENERATE IDEAS AND THE POWER TO IMPLEMENT THEM

I keep hearing the same story, the same dilemma: "I had the exact same idea, and now someone else has gone and done it. That's my success this person is celebrating now!" No, it's not, Captain Careless, because you didn't put the idea into practice. You sat down in the Lamborghini, but you didn't turn the key in the ignition.

For far too many brilliant ideas, the ignition key is never turned; the machine simply sits, no miles are traveled. The big misunderstanding is thinking the idea is ready after you have merely thought it through. Boom! Wrong. The work actually does start when you've thought your idea through, but this work is still largely in your head, not on the ground. Of course, you have to go out and make an effort, but hey, that has hopefully been clear. (You're reading a business book here and not Harry Potter!)

On the following pages, we'll look at the processes that need to be in your mind, in order for you to remain productive, effective, and on course for the long-term realization of your next killer idea. Your thoughts create your actions.

10 SUPER-PERFORMANCE METHODS

If you're not going full speed, your ideas are just daydreams—quite nice at the next dinner party if you want to talk about all your great ideas that someone else has implemented. The good news is that I have put together ten highly tactical performance methods that help me to really move the needle. Step on the gas! As an overview, you can consider these ten "bullets" to be like the field players of a strong soccer team. Everyone has to play together, pull their own weight, and be in their position so that the ball will move properly and you'll have a realistic chance of winning. But without these ten teammates on the pitch, there's no game.

First, a short disclaimer and some personal advice from me: Yes, you will need every single element from this series (100 percent, my friend). But don't make yourself crazy! No one is asking you to turn your whole life around by tomorrow. That would only lead to chaos.

The best football team trains for years, until they start to work their magic. Just start to build these valuable new strategies and tactics into your everyday life, piece by piece. Relax. Take it easy!

Really make it your goal to do these things with iron discipline and inexhaustible willpower, every day, again and again, until they become as automatic as brushing your teeth or shifting gears in a car! (More about this in Method #6.) I promise you this now (and please think of me when the time comes): When you begin to follow and live these strategies, you will feel something you have never felt before in your life. A sense of fulfillment and pride, of satisfaction and strength that will fill you completely from within. This is really (no bullshit) absolute madness! As a would-be biologist, I can tell you that this feeling is caused by the neurotransmitter dopamine, a healthy drug. Get high on it!

1. FLOW AND MEDITATION

Do you know that feeling when everything you do just works? Maybe it happens in a good conversation, when you're funny and quick-witted, and have all the answers at the ready. Or maybe it happens in sports, when you hit every basket, or score on every slapshot, or out-dance opponents like Lionel Messi. This kind of moment, this feeling, is called "flow." You have flow when you don't think about what you're doing, when it just happens. It's much more subconscious, than conscious. (Remember how much faster your subconscious mind is moving!) You do everything easily, the universe is in balance, and everything is cool. We will now dissect this feeling to understand its individual elements in order to make the "flow" experience happen in any situation.

THE SUBCONSCIOUS

Let's start with the subconscious. Try not to think! Can't do it, right? Why? Because you are still consciously thinking, "Don't think!" To help you get to your subconscious, you should, instead, think about meditation. No, not about Eastern mystics sitting cross-legged, but about the modern meditators: the Silicon Valley tech billionaires, the top athletes, the world's creative elite, writers, actors, crazy Paint-Party® developers, and other lunatics. All these folks meditate up to twice per day. One of my great role models for creative thinking is Tim Ferriss (timferriss.com). During his podcast, he asks his guests about their morning routines, and almost everyone answers that they do meditation or some other kind of introspection every morning.

Meditation helps get you out of your consciousness and into your feelings, into your immediacy, your being—into the subconscious. It relaxes you and releases tension. You feel like a newborn.

It's best to start out with a guided meditation, such as one by Tara Bach (tarabach.com), or via an app called "Headspace" (headspace.com). Let yourself go and enjoy the programmed journey. When you return to yourself, you are completely at peace, you are one with yourself, and it will feel rejuvenatingly good. This kind of meditative relaxation (performed in the morning) sends you into the new day both strengthened and full of energy. You are ready; you are there. You no longer chase your thoughts; you become an observer and a conscious decision-maker. You have control: your brain is a wild horse that you have tamed, for now. You'll gain an uncanny productivity and have a smart advantage over anyone who just stumbles into the day without a starting concept or routine. Your team already plays systematically, with clever moves and tactics. But don't just start off running, start calmly! The strength lies in the calm.

2. JOURNAL OF JOY

"The year has gone by so fast; I don't even know where it went!" Does this phrase sound familiar to you? Me, too! Time flies, and with it go all the moments and situations, good and bad. Hours become days, days become months, and months become years—so quickly that every year we become more frightened that another year is already over. It seems that every year, the clock hands spin a little bit faster.

What a pity. In this hamster wheel of appointments and deadlines, we forget all the small beautiful moments of real fulfillment that have made us feel really good. The machine just keeps on running, unstoppable. However, I have found a diary is a good way to record and document what I have experienced, although I'm more interested in the emotions than in the details of the experience.

Think back to the really great moments in your life, to the real highlights full of happiness and joy. Take yourself back to these places and relive the situation. It's not so much about remembering the action or the details, but about that warm feeling in your stomach. Your high school graduation, your first kiss with a person you really loved, and who really made you tingle. Yes, keep a diary, but a diary of your joy. Your life flies past you, so keep these key moments firmly in your heart. Write them down to remember and enjoy them. This reflection will remind you how happy and satisfied you actually are, and why. This inner dialogue, your very personal introspection, is the basis for real happiness and your best life. I am not a fan of spiritual wishy-washiness—honest. But I'm now going to give you some concrete and unadulterated questions that are food for thought, and which I consider for myself every morning after getting up and every evening before going to bed. This ritual has become like an addiction; I promise you that you will feel really good afterwards, and never want to change back again.

Get a notebook, and write down the answers to the following questions, every morning and every evening. (This stuff is not mine, by the way, but has long been recommended by personality development gurus of ages—because it works!)

WHAT AM I THANKFUL FOR?

Write down everything you can think of, but focus on what you would otherwise take for granted. Your family, friends, your health and theirs, your home, the weather, tasty food, the self-improvement books you can read, and the endless potentials and possibilities that each new day brings. It's focusing on the simple things that makes you realize how important they are to you, and sets the course for a day of gratitude, fulfillment, happiness, and contentment. Write things down, and smile—with your lips, with your eyes, with your heart! There is so much you can be grateful for: enjoy it and hold onto it tightly because then it will hold onto you!

WHAT AM I PROUD OF?

You accomplish something—every day! What are you really proud of? You should appreciate it and pat yourself on the back! Well done! Keep up the good work! You've earned this positive feedback and hearing it helps to make sure you're on track so that you celebrate success every day. Here, it's not about world-changing achievements or heroic deeds. It's about the little things you keep doing that make you really proud. The kind words you said to a stranger today, your discipline that drives you to the gym every day, the healthy meal you prepared, your ambitious goals, the fears that you have overcome, and those that you will overcome. Every day, there are so many skills and choices that make you special and unique! Make consciously good choices, consciously take the right path (the little voice in your heart always knows which one is the right path), and be proud of yourself! Document your pride and enjoy it. You want to experience this joy again and again so that you find yourself automatically doing things that make you proud again and again. This upward spiral can help you achieve the greatest goals of your best life—guaranteed, without pressure, but with a lot of joy in your own pride.

WHO DID I HELP TODAY? WHO CAN I HELP TODAY?

When your hand is open to give, it is also open to receive. One of my greatest "Aha!" experiences was when I realized that, as long as I am helping other people get what they need, I am happy, fulfilled, and abnormally successful. My events exploded because I gave people the feelings and emotions that they wanted. The people go crazy, the event is successful, everyone wins, and the world is fine!

Concentrate on this fundamental logic as you consider your next steps. Who did I help today? And who can I help today? Start small: a compliment, a helping hand, support, good advice. Helping feels unbelievably good for you. It goes with the person you helped out into the world and always returns exponentially—with a grand flourish. When you provide help, good things happen—guaranteed. This is how the world works; it's actually quite simple. Record how you help others in your "Journal of Joy," and notice how this daily journaling prepares you for a day filled with meaning, purpose and happiness. End your day with the same energy: as you close your eyes, you should be bursting with fulfillment and with anticipation for the next day of your dreams. You will feel the most beautiful joy and, above all, the joy that will get you out of bed early.

THE HAND THAT GIVES SOMETHING, RECEIVES SOMETHING IN RETURN!

3. FITNESS

The time when weight training was associated with machismo is undoubtedly over. Fitness is one of the best productivity tools available. I'm not a physical education teacher, but for as long I can remember, I've been on the move, and sports have been an essential part of my life. No matter what happens, you're always a winner if you at least have sports in your everyday life—even if everything else goes wrong. The barbells don't care; their honest feedback and your feeling of having achieved something will be there for you every day!

If you want to impress the skeptics and your buddies, simply say that short physical training (for example, twenty push-ups) releases endorphins, dopamine, and serotonin (which we've already discussed)— shooting you immediately into orbit, both physically and mentally. You'll feel good, strong, healthy, productive, well-balanced, and, at the same time, you'll improve your physique and general health.

Specific examples: there are lots of training plans, and every gym rat will tell you about their very own routine, special plan, or eccentric tip. But the first important point: you're in the gym to train, and the whole thing only makes sense if you don't break the continuity and routine. If you decide to go lifting three times a week, be in the gym three times a week, with no excuses! Your date with the gym is at least as important as your date in the bar, or any other social excuse. Never miss a session again! Get a training plan that works for you, that is adapted to your body and your goals, that you can adhere to, and that makes sense. Please don't let some bull-neck from the gym tell you what you need to do. Instead, ask a personal trainer. This is very important! You don't ask the guy with the most expensive set of wheels how to drive a car. The driving instructor explains that to you quite well.

Buy some good equipment: a cool outfit feel comfortable in, good shoes, and gloves (if you want to do some heavy lifting). There's no point in dragging yourself to the gym in an old outfit you got for a class at the community center or in a faded Chicago Bulls jersey from the '90s with Michael Jordan's name on the back. You have to feel good when you look in the mirror. Transfer this line of thinking to other areas besides the gym. For example, invest in a high-quality mattress, really good blankets, pillows and sheets. Muscles grow during your resting phase. First-class sleep creates a first-class life! Have music that motivates you! Spotify playlists and podcast apps are a good idea. In this way, you can always change whatever is streaming into your ears. There's nothing more demotivating than always hearing the same music, so keep it fresh! Buy some decent headphones and get focused!

While this may sound like "painting-by-numbers" fitness, I am absolutely serious! Not that I'm an expert, but it's important to me that you keep going until your fitness training becomes a routine and an integral part of your life. Why? Because I've seen the benefits for myself. The balance, the joy, the look, and the energy you get from training help make you capable of tackling anything that might come up in your business. I can't promise that going to the gym will make you a millionaire, but I *can* assure you that your mindset will be turned completely inside out!

DON'T MAKE EXCUSES. MOVE!

What makes fitness so exciting for me—besides the improvement in mindset, discipline, health, and performance—are the crystal-clear parallels fitness training has to your thriving business and your best life! We are each solely responsible for lifting weights, creating things, and making progress. There's a clear correlation between the amount of weight and the muscle gain—an inter-dependence between discipline and result. Other important variables in this formula are nutrition, rest periods, intervals, plans, regularity, and ambition. Whoever lifts a lot at the gym gets a lot in return. If you keep lifting weights that make your body strain, your muscles will develop. To put it simply, your muscles get the following message: "We have to lift more than we can at the moment, so we have to grow."

Mens sana
in corpore sano

100%

ABS
are made in the kitchen

QUICK TIP

My fascination with optimizing process and maximizing results led me to design a training plan that guaranteed me all the benefits of a regular strength-training routine, while making the best possible use of my time in the gym. For instance, I am never at the gym for longer than forty-five to sixty minutes, and I arrive already in my workout clothes.

Here's the essential idea for your "next big thing": demand more from yourself than you can and want right now, and you will have to evolve!

Your assistant: a training partner. Have you ever watched people help each other at the gym? The last repetitions with heavy weights—the ones that really hurt, the ones that count—are always done in pairs. A training partner helps to secure the weight and motivate you. For your best life, find a training partner who is there for you when you lift a heavy weight, who helps you, who protects you, and who believes in you. So if you don't yet have a training partner, put this book away. Get a gym membership, call your best friend, and take them with you! The gym represents many next big things in life and business. Guaranteed!

IN CONCRETE TERMS, HERE'S MY STRATEGY

- 6 times per week in the gym

- 2 "3-day split" = 6 sessions (a classic 3-day workout split is done twice per week, Sundays are free)

- All exercises are done in "super sets" to shorten the training time by up to 50 percent (in the break from exercise A, you do exercise B)

- 3 to 4 exercises per muscle, with 3 to 4 sets and approximately 8 to 10 repetitions per muscle

- Use the "push-pull" principle (exercise A = push, exercise B = pull)

- Use "antagonist training" (exercise A = biceps, exercise B = triceps)

- In 90 percent of the exercises, select a weight so that 8 to 10 repetitions are possible

- In 10 percent of the exercises, select a weight so that only 4 to 6 repetitions are possible, and extend the "cadence times" (duration that the muscle is under tension; one repetition lasts approximately 8 seconds). Rest/pause sets can also be inserted (one repetition at maximum force, 5 to 10 seconds pause, one repetition at maximum force). Repeat this sequence about 5 to 6 times

A lot of myths circulate about abdominal exercises, but the abdominal muscles are just like any other muscle. Anyone who does hundreds of crunches is doing something wrong, just the same as you can't do 100 bicep curls without something being wrong.

HERE IS MY ROUTINE

- Only 3 crunches and approximately 20 repetitions

- Hang and use the weight of the legs (lifting your legs is much harder than lifting your chest and head, and relies less on the back)

- Lift both straight out and then to the sides

The big secret is discipline. Simply never miss a training session again and nothing will stand in the way of your dream figure. That's it! The rest is a product of your diet. Your health and body are 90 percent based on what you eat, and only 10 percent on what you do in the gym.

4. NUTRITION

Let me paint a scenario for you. Your diet is a complete mess: chocolate, fries, hamburgers, ice cream, too much of everything and, above all, the wrong things. You order this stuff because it makes you feel satisfied and fulfilled (in the truest sense of the word). You want to chow down so badly, so alright, let's go! And afterwards? You always— every single time—feel sick. You feel like you're going to vomit, you're much too full, tired, and just *done*. Your cholesterol and blood sugar levels are rising. For a moment, your body is poisoned.

We all recognize this scenario. But now comes my question, "Why do you keep doing it?" Kind of crazy, isn't it? Here's my tip: the feelings that you want from a really good meal ("good" is often confused with "a lot") require food of the best quality. Imagine driving a sports car. You want to put the pedal to the metal, but the wrong gas is in the tank! That won't work. It's gotta be top notch, high octane—really good stuff. Good for the transmission, for longevity, for well-being. I know guys who just shovel cheap rubbish into their cars' mouths but polish their wheel rims with a cleaning product so special that 100 milliliters costs more than 20 liters of freshly squeezed orange juice. What's wrong with that?

Make it clear to yourself that your body reacts immediately to what you provide it. Every single little bit that goes into your body is evaluated, applied, and has an effect—even if it just destroys and poisons. (And hopefully, we don't have to talk about drugs or cigarettes here. Come on!) An important note for the critics who say that it would be too expensive to live healthily: This is a total paradox. Save a little cash by living like a human garbage can, and die a lot sooner. And in the meantime, you feel like shit. Bravo, well done, Mr. Cheapskate!

The trick is not just quality, but also quantity and routine. Not knowing what you want to eat leads to wasted time and money in the supermarket. I eat maybe four to five different dishes in different variations—all affordable, prepared ultra-fast—without getting a lot of kitchen stuff dirty, and, since I know the route in the supermarket very well, the trips are super quick.

Learn what you need to feed your body every day in order to really feel well. In case you have no idea: lean meat, good fish, vegetables, olive oil, fruit, water, freshly squeezed juices, nuts, etc. Then come up with some nice recipes, and just follow your plan. The following should happen: you have more free time, fewer basics to think about, and you are healthy, lively, happy, and joyful because you are doing what's good for your body. This newly found energy—physical and mental—takes you to previously inaccessible places. You pivot faster, you're more alert, you look better, you are more active, and you want to go to the gym because you are taking responsibility for yourself. This extremely fast upward spiral begins with your shopping list. Eat clean, get smart, feel great—not just for yourself, but for your family!

EAT CLEAN, GET SMART, FEEL GREAT!

It has been scientifically proven that an unbalanced diet significantly increases the risk of heart disease and diabetes, especially for your children. Just one piece of healthy salmon per week reduces the risk of developing kidney cancer by more than 50 percent, and thus has a direct impact on your health. Think about tomorrow when you are hungry today! Imagine that your health is like a bank account. Some foods make you rich and increase your balance, while others rob the bank, threatening to drive you to bankruptcy (sometimes daily). Over time, bad food results in destructive patterns that make living a healthy lifestyle almost impossible. Break the patterns at the beginning of the chain and secure your account balance by making the right decisions. Thoughtful choices at the supermarket put the right contents in your fridge, which in turn lead to a healthy lifestyle. The first domino in your line of big decisions must fall properly, and then everything else happens organically, providing invaluable wealth to your health account!

RECIPES

I love cooking and taking the time to prepare and enjoy a nice meal. However, this is not a cookbook. For the sake of time, I will focus on informal and fast methods of preparing these recipe favorites. Quick and inexpensive, and super-healthy, they are ready in a few minutes, and they are really delicious. Sometimes, even efficiency tastes great!

BREAKFAST

MATTHEW'S MICROWAVE VEGGIE OMELETTE BOWL

You need: 4 egg whites, onion, tomato, spinach, and almond milk.

Stir ingredients together in a bowl coated with a little olive oil. Stick the bowl in the microwave and cook until the egg white thickens (about 1 minute). Let cool for 2 minutes and eat directly from the bowl. Serve with fresh pressed orange juice.

For a vegan alternative: You can create a pretty amazing (in terms of texture and taste) "vegan egg" by using coconut milk, corn flour, miso paste, and Indian black salt (Kala Namak). Just check out my buddy Gas Oakley on YouTube to see how it's made.

LUNCH

MATTHEW'S SALMON PLATE

You need: Red beets, lemon, sea salt, 2 slices of black bread, olive oil, and salmon (ready-to-eat, e.g., smoked or hot-smoked salmon).

Add the oil and lemon juice to the beets, season with sea salt, add bread and salmon, and eat directly from the plate.

For a vegan alternative: Substitute for the salmon this vegan burger packed with plant protein. The patty is made by blending the "meat" of an oven roasted sweet potato with mixed beans and some oats. Just blend for a few pulses; don't make a paste or the mixture won't hold together. Form patties with your hands, dusted with flour, so mixture doesn't stick. Fry lightly on both sides in a pan with olive oil, and then oven roast at 180 degrees Celsius, until the desired firmness. Serve on a whole wheat burger, with some avocado, tomato, and your choice of greens.

SNACK

MATTHEW'S PROTEIN SHAKE

You need: Water, honey, raspberries, blueberries, walnuts, ice cubes, and 50 g protein powder (plant protein, whey, or whatever you favor).

Blend everything, and drink directly from the mixer. Try using almond or coconut milk, and maybe add some oats if you want a bold texture.

DINNER

MATTHEW'S CHICKEN SALAD BOWL

You need: Tomatoes, onion, lettuce mix, basil, chicken breast (pre-cooked), sunflower seeds, avocado, and olive oil.

Chop everything, put it in the bowl, sprinkle sunflower seeds, drizzle olive oil on top, and eat directly from the bowl.

For a vegan alternative: Use tofu or tempeh as the protein source. If you're allergic to soy, use chickpeas or red lentils (they have as much protein as a can of tuna).

Besides protein powder, the only food supplement I currently use is organically bound sulfur, in the form of methylsulfonylmethane (MSM). Sulfur is ultra-important for the body, and often dangerously underestimated. The human body contains five times more sulfur than magnesium, and forty times more sulfur than iron. I hear everywhere about magnesium and iron supplements, but nobody talks about sulfur. However, in the body, hardly any process takes place without sulfur. It's important for the development of vital antioxidants and hormones. If you're interested, google it!

For those who want to dive deeper into the mystical world of diet theory—sorry, I'm the wrong person to ask! :) I keep my explanations simple, not because I was bad in biology, but because the many diet fads have become confusing. So go for what's quick and easy. Don't exceed your minimum calorie requirement and reduce carbohydrates in the evening. That's it!

Okay, I'd feel guilty if I left this one out, so here's one more tip. Take it or leave it! I openly admit that I've never tried it myself, but (according to my research), the following diet package seems waterproof, and many of my fitness friends and lateral thinkers (like Tim Ferriss) swear by it. Lo and behold:

THE KETOGENIC DIET

It's a medical way of describing the low-carb diet: lots of fat, medium protein, very few carbohydrates. We turn the conventional food pyramid around 180 degrees and do the opposite of a conventional diet (except we still use fish). When we question conventional wisdom, we can definitely expect quite different results. How it works: Carbohydrates from sugar are completely eliminated (which also a therapeutic approach for the treatment of childhood epilepsy, so it's not that unusual). While energy is normally gained by the metabolism of carbohydrates into glucose, the ketogenic diet no longer draws its energy requirements from glucose. Instead, it draws energy only from fat, so glucose's end-products build up in the body—the ketone bodies. This condition is called ketosis—an impressive, technical-sounding word, but it has a clear takeaway: this diet burns fat, and lots of it!

If the ketogenic diet intrigues you, then check it out. I added it here only as a handy tip.

5. THE WINNER'S ROUTINE

"What a great day!" When was the last time you said that, and why? We're all familiar with that type of day: we do a lot, everything runs smoothly, things work out, and at the end of this excellent day, we simply feel good. These days feel so good that I've meticulously broken down this feeling into its individual components and into its exact "triggers" so that I'm able to reproduce it! I am now addicted to this feeling, to the sense of having really engaged with something, of having really used the day and its full potential! But don't forget: sometimes it's equally important to maximize your downtime to help you refuel for the next up-cycle. Be flexible in the way you do it. Rigid trees break in a storm while flexible trees, like palms, withstand any hurricane. How they do it? They simply *bend*. Don't force anything, but flow and be flexible.

One crucial finding is that there is a routine at the heart of your best day. Everyone has such a routine, including you. Like going to the gym, there's a plan, an exact schedule for your best day. Certain things have to happen for you to feel really good. The more elements you can identify from your winning routine, the more effectively you can reproduce the feeling of a really well-lived day. We'll consider both fixed and flexible elements here. You need some of these routines every day; you need others only in certain circumstances.

First, we'll look at the fixed elements. Let's start with the morning. To feel good, how early do you have to get up? You may not want to hear this, but the earlier you get up, the better you'll feel. Sorry, buddy! But let's be honest: You always want to accomplish the best things as soon as possible. Waiting takes time and nerves, shifting the moment of satisfaction further and further away. You want to be the first to reach the goal, the first to pass the finish line. How? By being faster than everyone else! But be careful. Speeding through your efforts is always at the expense of efficiency. Faster means more strenuous. Faster means more dangerous. Faster means less careful. Faster means less attention to doing a good job. You don't have to go any faster than needed, as long as you live your best life and have a winning routine.

A key point: don't try to do more things in the same amount of time in order to reach your goal faster. Just start earlier than everyone else. The success of your best possible life depends on doing the things that others don't want to do. That's your advantage.

Your new strategy should include utilizing the time between five and seven in the morning. These two hours are your advantage, your pole position. Using these two hours sharpens your focus and thoughts, without any additional effort.

Quite simply, whoever sleeps less is awake more. You start the race two hours earlier.

QUICK TIP

Keep a bowl of cold water and a cloth next to your bed. As soon as your alarm clock rings, sit down, soak the cloth and wipe your face. Then drink a glass of water, and the probability that you will lie down again decreases by up to 90 percent. Every day, we have the opportunity to be 100 laps ahead of everyone else if we simply start earlier.

At the Olympics, false starts are declared if one runner begins just one millisecond earlier than the others—giving them an unfair advantage. But in our best lives, there are small gaps in the rules that will give us a fair advantage.

The following are two important drivers:

THE MISSION

You need to know exactly why you're getting up. Have a plan; lay out your clothes ahead of time—maybe for the gym. You need to immediately know where you're going. Structure and plans create your next steps.

THE FEELING

Everybody's been up at five o'clock before. The feeling of peace, the feeling of being active while alone in a world that's still asleep, the feeling of starting earlier, of getting a better start, of being more relaxed while no one else is on the track—it all feels great! This unique feeling helps connect you to your best life. While everyone is still asleep, you're already running the first laps of a race that now you can't lose.

So, Element Number 1 of your fixed winning routine: get up early! But how? Go to bed early! (This also helps nail down your evening plans, at least on weekdays.) Honestly, what are you thinking, watching some trash on TV until two or three in the morning? (Hopefully, you've already sold the TV.) That kind of evening has no added value; it's a waste of time, life, and potential growth. Element Number 2: no TV!

And that brings us to Element Number 3: reading and learning. You should read or learn something new every day. The time before going to bed is very suitable. Never close your eyes until you've read for 30 minutes (inspiring reading, no trash). This element is followed by the world's best thinkers and entrepreneurs. The last thoughts you place into your brain before you go to sleep should be of the highest quality. Your subconscious will spend the whole night with these thoughts, so please don't waste the opportunity on cheap B-movies or embarrassing late-night action films. Always have a good book next to your bed. Always. No, it's not expensive: for less than a few bucks on Amazon, you can get into the heads of the most interesting personalities in the world, *and* the books will be delivered to your door. Do it!

Subdivide your best day into active and reactive periods. When do you act, and when do you react? When are you a doer, and when are you a manager?

MY APPROACH

Until noon, I'm a doer. No emails, no calls, no social networks. It's all about me, and I make the rules to benefit myself. Gym, creative work, writing, reading.

Starting at noon, I'm a manager. To-do lists, emails, phone calls. From this point on, external people have access to my schedule, and I manage this access. The administrative and management work always comes with a tradeoff because it taxes my cognitive abilities. Every output during this time is always at the expense of creativity and attention. Schedule this period precisely, and give it a time limit, so you don't squander your cognitive savings. Your tasks will always take as long as the time you schedule, so set clear timeframes to work in a focused way!

DON'T WASTE YOUR TIME, FRIEND!

SOME NO-BRAINERS THAT SHOULD NOT BE MISSED ON YOUR BEST DAY

- Exercise

- Healthy nutrition, period

- Remember to separate Creation vs. Reaction. Understand which activities are creative (writing, conceptualizing, working creatively), and which ones are reactive (phone, email). Then separate these activities from each other, and reserve the creative things for a time of the day when you have maximum strength, both mentally and physically! You can still react when you're drained

- Be honest. Honesty, authenticity toward yourself and your fellow humans.

- Help others. Can you remember a situation in which you were able to really help someone? This indescribable feeling, this warmth in the stomach, is definitely a fixed component of a top-notch day. Help someone, be kind to a stranger, give, share, and you'll get back more than you've given—always!

Safeguard your time! Don't waste any of it, honestly. Your time is your most valuable resource. Unrecoverable. For instance, I am wasting time when I do something that I know I shouldn't be doing. For example, if I need to go exercise or to work on my project, but instead I'm on YouTube or Facebook, I'm aware that I'm not using my time well. But I don't think it's a waste of time to watch a movie to have fun if I know that there's nothing more important to be done at that moment.

SOME PRODUCTIVITY STRATEGIES AND TOOLS FOR MAXIMIZED BENEFITS IN THE SHORTEST POSSIBLE TIME

- Increase the speed (response rate) of the mouse/trackpad on your PC/laptop. Your mouse hand travels many "miles" every day, so this simple adjustment should more than double your speed. (Tip: Try increasing the speed to twice your usual. The first few minutes will seem strange, but your brain will get used to it very quickly.)

- Get an appointment app! If you plan a lot of meetings, you know how much valuable time is lost in the eternal back and forth. An app like "Schedule Once" helps a lot. Additionally, when proposing meetings, it's helpful to always suggest three possible dates. Doing that will help prevent date selection from turning into an email war.

- Do it now! Don't put easy-to-accomplish things on hold—do them now! That way, you save the attention and energy needed to re-schedule them. When you bypass your tendency toward laziness, the psychological ROI (Return on Investment) is immense. For example, I make my bed every morning, a habit I owe to my grandma. She used to say "Always put everything away, and above all, always in the same place. Then you will never have to search again in your life."

- Sort the money in your wallet! Not only out of respect for your money, but also for order and efficiency. Arrange bills by amount and always in the same direction—it feels great, looks great, makes counting easier, and keeps you grounded.

Regard your values and visions as part of your winning routine! People have often sought the true meaning of life—but they would be hard-pressed to find a simple "truth-of-all-truths." In reality, life's meaning can be understood in terms of your winning routine: a kind of root with many branches, many elements, and various "arms" that reinforce you, and give you strength. Your personal "meaning of life" is based on your emotions, your values, goals, and ideals, and is summarized by your regular rituals and your own winning routine!

In your routine, new things can be added and others subtracted. Always dynamic and in motion, the process of developing and maintaining your routine anchors you deeper and deeper into the earth of your environment, and, on hard days, protects you from the storms.

And now, on to the flexible elements of your winning routine: What must happen in your life? What people must especially be there for you right now? Which projects are hot, and what is really important? All these questions belong in timeframes, just like the fixed elements of your winning routine. Do them, and feel good about them until they are completed. The flexible elements of your winning routine come and go. At times, there will be super-important projects, so your routine will involve working on them daily. The focus here is on maintaining continuity.

Exceptionally gifted individuals lose some of their mystique when their abilities are dissected. I am giving you a systematic breakdown of what is required. Through discipline, planning, perseverance, and will, you, too, can do anything. Just include this in your winning routine: plan exactly what needs to happen—and when—in order to make yourself happy and fulfilled, and then let your system make it happen. Like in a perfectly rehearsed play, just follow the script. You don't have to think much, just stick to your plan!

6. THE "WILLPOWER" MUSCLE

I mentioned earlier a scientific study that examined the brains of London taxi drivers, specifically the prefrontal cortex (the frontal lobe of the cerebral cortex, which is responsible for spatial imagination and navigation, among other things). London cabbies are in great demand for such research projects because the road network in London is impudently complex, and scientists like to examine the structure of such "human road maps." The results were astonishing. Most of the taxi drivers had a physically larger prefrontal cortex compared to the prefrontal cortices of subjects with "normal" knowledge of London's street layout. The ability of the brain to grow is called "neuroplasticity." An absolutely incredible and groundbreaking notion! No one should ever again say, "I can't learn this, I was born stupid!" Not only can you learn everything, but—regardless of the brain you were born with— you can train your brain like a muscle and make it really fit and strong (in the truest sense of the word). In other words, you can train your brain regularly as if it were a bicep by flexing it and properly building up mass! Okay, so far this as all awesome, but now it's going to get really crazy.

The prefrontal cortex, which we have just learned is trainable, is also responsible for human willpower. From now on, let's call it the "Willpower Muscle" and that aspect can get strengthened, too. What would happen if your Willpower Muscle really had some drive? How early would you get out of bed in the morning? How often would you go to the gym? How would your projects go, your relationships, your friendships? What about your goals and dreams?

66 DAYS TO A NEW ROUTINE

More willpower is the basis of all good results, and your brain is trainable. Don't stop reading now, because I'm giving you the key to a system that, however hard, will allow you to burn every new routine into your best life in less than three months.

It will become so ingrained that afterwards you won't have to use any willpower at all because, from that point on, everything will just run by itself—automatically. Like for a child learning to walk, only the first steps are difficult. The rest will "run" without you having to think about it. In sixty-six days! It takes sixty-six days to get a new routine into your life. This is scientifically proven. You want to be able to get up every day at five o'clock? Then pull it off sixty-six times, and it will happen on its own. You want to hit the gym five times a week? Sixty-six days, and then you do it automatically, guaranteed.

Automation is the keyword. You train your prefrontal cortex, your Willpower Muscle, on a specific task for sixty-six days—just like at the gym—until it's really fit. Then the automation process takes over, and you don't have to use any more willpower. Your "muscle" has grown enough, the routine is now part of your life, and you are strong enough to do it without much willpower, automatically. So take a breath and see what that means: no matter what you can do or want to do, everything is possible with the right system and a well thought-out action plan! Tick off every day on the calendar when you have done exactly what you wanted to do, and then see how you climb to the top in no time at all. Using this exact sixty-six-day tactic, I made myself and my willpower fit enough to finish this book in record time—a few paragraphs every day—until my Willpower Muscle became so strong, that I didn't even have to think about whether I would write or not. It simply happened.

And now, a mega-thought regarding your decision-making power, which depends on your willpower. These two must play together, just like a quarterback and a defensive line in football. Imagine that each day you have only a finite number of really good decisions that you can make—say one hundred. The more decisions you spend on seemingly important, but actually trivial things (what I wear, what I post on Facebook, what I cook today, etc.), the fewer decisions you have left for the really important things. Save your few decisions by putting everything irrelevant on autopilot. Why do you think world-class thinkers like (the late) Steve Jobs always wear the same clothes? Why do they always eat the same things? These guys know all about automation, knowing it can allow them to have a "full storeroom" available whenever they need to make the important decisions that move them forward, that help grow their prefrontal cortex, that lead them to their best lives—decisions that make them proud and happy.

So the takeaway is this: The part of your brain that is responsible for willpower (prefrontal cortex), can be trained by doing again and again—at least sixty-six days in a row—the things you want to anchor in your life, and that you need in order to grow and be fulfilled. You'll succeed by conserving your finite number of decisions and not blowing them on bullshit, only springing into action when doing so will really help you.

Conversely, this also means the following: the more options you consider, the less fulfillment will result, because your options may exhaust by the time you need to make your decisions.

Tim Ferriss—lateral thinker, author, investor, and a true master of analyzing seemingly unfathomable elite performance and complex ways of thinking—repeatedly talks in his blog (www.tim.blog) about this question: Which is more important—a better result with less fulfillment, or a worse result with more fulfillment? Let's be practical.

Would you rather weigh and compare options for months, and then doubt your decision for months? Or would you rather decide more quickly, even if the quality is up to 20 percent lower, and feel confident knowing that a quick decision is more efficient?

What is better, and by what guidelines is this measured?

We assess the "optimal" option by its practicability. In theory, your initial financial situation can always be restored, but time, nerves, and attention never are. Attention and nerves—just like your decisions— are finite values that are consumed by even a brief engagement with a problem, even if you don't actively pay attention. Here's an example: How well can you sleep if you hear about a serious problem shortly before going to bed, something that you can't solve until the next morning? You don't actively address the problem, but your attention and nervous reserves are subconsciously and passively being used. You ponder, and you make decisions. The time slept this night remains unchanged, but your attention and decision-making power is reduced, reducing the value of the time. In other words, you can't sleep, so when you get up the next morning, you're useless (empty, in the truest sense of the word).

It's important not to start new trains of thought until you are ready to react immediately to the potential problems. Too many options always cost dearly in units of time, decision-making power, and attention, which means that these time units are no longer available for implementation, awareness, and action. Too many options pull you out of the moment. Too much choice always has a negative impact on productivity, fulfillment, and satisfaction. Conclusion: having too many options makes you less productive and increases your pressure to make quality decisions, which eventually results in doubt.

But increased costs due to artificially reduced options should be seen as a credit—an investment in time, nerves, and fulfillment. They result in time saved by preventing decisions that might be regretted later. Clear directions and rules help structure and limit the options, thus increasing productivity and satisfaction. Your own rules in your personal and business environment will facilitate the decision-making process by making it solely depend on measurable, recognizable factors.

Automate your decisions and find the rhythm of your winning routine. Set up standing orders, direct debit authorizations, and sign subscription contracts for the things you need regularly: my toothpaste and razor blades, for instance, are delivered to me. Eliminate unnecessary decisions and avoid shifting problems or postponing the moment of decision! It's better to cancel your date and surprise them if you find you can actually make it, than it is to agree to come knowing you probably won't, simply to avoid saying no.

What's at stake? The worst case is the risk of creating a negative result that can't be repaired. If the risk is low, you can maximize efficiency and conserve resources to simply decide things and move on. The requirements can provide a framework for facilitating the decision. One variable is the number of options: I will not consider more than ten. A time variable: I will not compare offers for longer than 24 hours. Or a monetary variable: if the risk of potential, immutable damage does not exceed $1,000, then I will decide immediately, without considering any further options.

Even if it sounds paradoxical—and we've talked about how new impressions can break your routine and help create ideas—routine can also enable creativity! Routines to increase effectiveness are valuable. You should make a clear distinction between the two. If you want to interrupt your usual routine for the sake of enjoyment or creativity, a walk or a vacation can be effective. The Winning Routine itself is always independent of location. So, you can always combine creativity with a clean, productive rhythm.

By the way, the best decisions are made in the morning (of course, because you still have so many decisions left). So get up early and knock out the very important things first. Let's go! Set your alarm clock!

7. YOU GET ALL THE THINGS YOU FOCUS ON

"Why me? Why can't I just get it?" Have you ever asked yourself these questions? Never do that again! Why? Asking them invites you to focus on finding as many reasons as possible that explain why you are incapable of doing something. And believe me, your brain is opinionated. You'll immediately get a lot of really good reasons that prove how incapable you suspect you are. Think a bit further down the road. What happened the last time you faced the same challenge? Exactly! All those reasons are immediately recalled. "Why should anything be better this time around? Well, I'd better leave it alone, and not proceed a step further."

You always get exactly what you focus on. If you ask yourself why something's not working, it's not going to work. It's as simple as that. But see what happens if you just change the question. Consider where you have been focusing your subconscious on (point five in my thoughts about creativity), and then work at the speed of light on a solution—on the "next steps." For instance, when you ask yourself "What would it mean for my development if I learned as much as possible from this situation?" or "How much more would it benefit me if I didn't stop now, but worked continuously on myself and my project, regardless of what happens?" Good questions always lead to good answers. Focus on growth, opportunities, big goals, and impressive developments, and that's exactly what will happen. When you truly focus on and believe in yourself, your thoughts become reality. How do you start believing in yourself? Ask your brain good questions, and let it answer. Prove to yourself that your goals can become reality and win the argument with your own doubts. Convince yourself of your growth, and it will happen all by itself!

People love stories, and that's why we tell them to each other, again and again, in response to all kinds of situations. The problem (and as we'll see later, also a potential advantage) is that we write our stories ourselves. The main drawback is that they are always biased, even though they may seem accurate to us. Here's an example. Your new partner on the project team seems closed off to you. Because you're confused, the storytelling inside your head begins: "Did I do something wrong? No, I'm not doing anything wrong. Or maybe I did? Maybe because I was ten minutes late to the meeting yesterday? Possibly. But then that would make him really petty because he himself was late last week. Why was that? Perhaps he's having an affair. Does he even have a wife? I don't know. Does he think I'm having an affair, and is that why he's keeping his distance? Okay, so he's implying that I'm having an affair, and on top of that, he's petty. It was only ten minutes."

STOP PLAYING MOVIES INSIDE YOUR HEAD

We could spin around with this story forever. That's how our head works—great stories, but of little use. At least if you're not a crime writer.

To keep your mind open, and remain unbiased and fair, two things are very important. Distance yourself from stories. And stop replaying movies inside your head. Your best and wildest stories are always written before you have done anything in response to something that you have observed. This intermediate phase is filled by your imagination, and often doesn't need any facts. These stories are often in your favor, and the more you listen to them, the more you believe them. Here's a really simple trick: honestly ask yourself what's going on! The moment you notice yourself starting a story with an observation—a new thriller about things you can't explain—turn the wild thoughts off, and just ask this question! Maybe your partner on the team was a bit insecure because he's new and you've been there for a while. He'd like some help from you, respects you immensely, but is also nervous about working with you. When you ask yourself what's going on, your insecure bubble bursts, and the two of you can write a much better—and, above all, real—story together!

I mentioned earlier that our stories can also have a huge advantage. After we've just completely shot down these stories, you may ask yourself "How so?" It's because we can use our stories to create a whole new response that becomes a lever for our happiness. You have the power to give every situation a meaning by using a story of your own choosing. There are Indian tribes in South America who celebrate whenever someone from their village dies. (I don't mean to make a religious digression; I just want to respectfully point out that these folks celebrate when someone dies.) They take a terrible situation and give it a different meaning that tells a different story.

Your stories create your emotions! Take your really difficult moments, your inexplicable setbacks, and use them to write a new story! The story of success must be built on hundreds of failures. Consider the story of the master, who needed every one of his mistakes before he could become what he is now. Or, the story of the relationship that must end in order for you to find the right person who is really meant for you. We don't necessarily get what we want—we get what we are and what we believe. Tell good stories, and they will become your truth. Take this truth with you into your everyday life. Minimize the effort you need to repent by refraining from complaining about yourself. Don't pay attention to your doubt! In concrete terms: if you don't complain for 24 hours, everything will change! For one day, you should refrain from any kind of complaint, doubt, negativity, or conscious disappointment. Complaints change nothing, but cost time, nerves, and attention. The time we spend criticizing the past and reliving it by complaining is poorly invested time, and will be lost forever.

Here's another tactical exercise for you to realize your best story. Every night before falling asleep, take five minutes to create in your mind a movie about your best life! Write the scenario in your head, in front of your mind's eye. Watch the film about yourself, and your role. Observe closely how you live your ideals, your values: full of integrity, truth, discipline, joy, love, and happiness. See for yourself how you do the things that make you proud, how you master situations the way you've always wanted, how you are the friend, partner, and person who corresponds to your deepest beliefs. Every evening, watch this film, *A*

Day in Your Best Life! Pay attention to every second and notice how this film becomes a reality when you get everything you really focus on.

8. SMILE

In the body, a simple smile produces endorphins and the "feel good" neurotransmitters—dopamine and serotonin—biologically (and verifiably) smoothing any social situation and helping you and the other person feel security, serenity, joy, and happiness. Have you heard the phrase, "He gave me a smile"? It's the bomb! Give everyone you meet a smile, immediately. I'm asking you to try this. You can't imagine how good you'll feel and how much positivity you'll get back. But here's the important thing: give a real smile, not a fake one! And don't just smile with your mouth: people will notice your reluctance immediately! A real smile is one that radiates from the inside, not from the outside.

A little tip: Before you smile, think about something beautiful or something funny. Don't just smile—laugh a little inside yourself. Then your eyes will laugh, too, and the smile will immediately be absolutely authentic. By the way, this is also a great tip for your next photo shoot. Imagine the photographer is naked, and you'll immediately have to laugh out loud. It works wonders, and the photo will be great!

9. SHOCK YOURSELF!

When was the last time you were really shocked? I'm not talking about the short moment of fright because your goofy friend unexpectedly said "Boo!" No, I mean a moment when you deliberately did something that really shook you up? You can create situations that turn your status quo completely on its head and thereby give you a breath of fresh air! Have you ever taken a wrong turn, and suddenly found yourself totally awake and present? Everything was crystal clear, and you were 100 percent functioning? We can create such moments and leverage them for maximum creativity, joy, power, and excitement! The next time your thoughts aren't really sharp and you feel burned out, shock yourself with something you wouldn't otherwise do. Go out, jump, scream, dance, and tell your body you're flipping a switch. You are changing the gears, and you want to keep moving forward! Everything old is suddenly washed away by the adrenaline rush, and now you're ready.

PRACTICAL, TACTICAL TIPS FOR EVERYDAY SITUATIONS THAT WILL IMMEDIATELY PUT YOU INTO TURBO MODE

- **Take a cold shower:** Totally easy, and you're just gonna fly out of the shower! I discovered this in Ibiza when our shower on the terrace had only cold water. The experience was incredibly positive every time. Try it—trust me!

- **Dance to the music:** Listen to loud music and dance for a moment as if no one was watching. Afterwards, you are guaranteed to be on a completely different level.

- **Give up a habit:** A victory over your bad behaviors will instantly shake you up—positively! Take a pass on a cigarette. Take another route home. Give up alcohol for thirty days. Don't look at your mobile for two hours. Triumph over your addictions, for that's where your victory march in life begins!

- **Adopt a winning attitude:** What pose do winners automatically make? Think of soccer players who score a goal, race car drivers on the victory podium, track and field athletes, or lottery winners: both arms up, head held high, looking up into the sky. Hold this pose for thirty seconds, and the body-spirit connection transports you immediately into completely different spheres. If you want to feel like a winner, first act like a winner!

- **Go for a walk:** Get out into the fresh air, into the woods or the field, and you'll be immediately ready for take-off. Combine this tip with listening to music and dancing, and there will be no stopping you!

- **"Study Music":** Search for that term on YouTube. I listen to this kind of music (which is supposed to improve concentration via alpha waves and binaural tonality) and can say it works! It'll be your new soundtrack that immediately changes everything.

- **Lie down for a minute:** Put your cell phone in airplane mode, put your legs up, and put your head down! Lie down for longer than thirty minutes and suddenly you're a new person.

- **Do the unexpected:** Don't let your body know what's gonna happen next. Surprise yourself often, and you'll be surprised by the results!

10. GO WHERE YOUR FEAR IS THE GREATEST!

New scientific studies show that the human brain wants to be challenged. We are really emotionally happy and satisfied when we grow, expose ourselves to new situations, celebrate successes, and when we rise above ourselves time and again. As Hafiz said, "You, yourself, are your own obstacle. Rise above yourself." It's not so hard to expand your own growth, but you have to go exactly where your greatest fear lies. You have to do exactly those things that make you really nervous, because that's when your feeling of success and your sense of victory over your own limitations will be at their highest.

YOUR FEAR SHOWS YOU THE WAY

Your potential and your growth require dealing with your fear and insecurity. Accept the invitation and walk through the fire, because you will always find your best life on the other side!

Remember your first kiss? The nervousness and insecurity? And yet you summed up all your courage and made a decision that changed your life forever. We have the greatest influence on our happiness and fulfillment during the moments of our biggest decisions! Direct your antennas toward your fear and run toward it as soon as you feel it.

Doing so will put you on the right track! You must do this again and again, with untiring perseverance, until you become really good at it.

Fear leads to perfection. How did we learn to read? In second grade, everyone had a book on the table and we took turns reading aloud, one kid after another. And what did we all do? We tried to anticipate which paragraph we would have to read ourselves, and then quietly in our heads, we reread the part thirty times, so that when it was our turn, we could read the thing out loud without any problems. So when we were seven years old, we already knew that we were motivated by the things that frighten us! We would never have read the paragraph thirty times voluntarily—at least not me, ha ha!

"YOU YOURSELF ARE YOUR OWN OBSTACLE, RISE ABOVE YOURSELF."

—HAFIZ

YOUR INNER CRITIC

Let's take a closer look at the concept of fear. Fear usually comes from making a worst-case fantasy about the consequences of your action (usually about something important to you). Fear is an inner voice that advises us against taking action. In her book *Playing Big*, Tara Mohr talks about the voice of the "inner critic," which manifests when we have faced fear and which expresses harmful self-criticism. This mechanism tries to provide emotional security by trying to protect us from being hurt by bad feedback from other people. So, the inner critic takes on the role of the raging mob, giving us bad criticism to try to prevent us from exposing ourselves to "dangerous" situations. Unfortunately, it's precisely these situations that determine our growth and success. This mechanism helps explain why a large part of humanity remains in mediocrity. Remember that your inner critic paradoxically wants to protect you by targeting the truly vulnerable areas of your psyche. From now on, always decide against its advice if you want to grow faster than you ever imagined. However, do use the inner critic's voice to discover your vulnerable areas (they are always the target of this criticism), and then try to engage directly with these weaknesses by writing them down or by talking to friends or family. Repurpose the inner critic's platform of attack and use it for your own growth.

There will be times when you're scared, when you're insecure, when you feel powerless, and when you can't seem to go anywhere. Moments like these just happen; they are totally normal. So talk to yourself now, in order to stay strong! Here's a really simple exercise that gives you more strength and fearlessness *immediately*. It consists of four sets of fifteen repetitions each. The basic idea comes from one of my greatest role models, Robin Sharma. (If you're unfamiliar with him, put this book aside for now, and go buy any of his books. Thank me later. This guy is amazing!)

Back to the four sets of fifteen repetitions each. It may sound like weightlifter jargon from the gym, but this exercise makes you immediately strong in your head and heart, not in your upper arms. Every day, morning and night, tell yourself the same sentence fifteen times. First in your head, then out loud, then in writing, and then out loud in front of the mirror. Choose a short sentence that makes you strong and corresponds to your deepest ideals and values. Something like, "I'm honest, authentic, fit and strong, and full of values and integrity." Choose your own very special sentence, and say it fifteen times in your head, fifteen times out loud, write it down once, and then say it fifteen times out loud in front of the mirror. You'll immediately notice how strong and fearless you feel. Do this exercise regularly! Never underestimate the power of your own words in the fight against your fears and sense of powerlessness. In order to grow, go to the place of your greatest fear on a daily basis, using the power of your words!

5

10 SYSTEMS FOR
WORLD-CLASS
LEADERSHIP

Since the very beginning of mankind, we have been fighting as individuals against the world's dangers. Going at it alone doesn't work very well, but working together dramatically increases the chance of survival. This is the reason for having a team and establishes the role of the leader. You're creative, the idea is in place, you have the right mindset, but now you have to make your team and shop thrive. But the problems that people face have changed. The Neanderthals had the brutal weather, the saber-toothed tiger, or the poisonous berries. Now, in the harsh jungle of the modern business world, we face global competition, the overwhelming speed of innovation, the eradication or turnover of entire business models within months, the unpredictable markets and share prices, as well as being part of a generation that cannot decide what to wear tomorrow, let alone what it wants from life, and what must be done to get it.

The danger today lies, above all, in perception. For the kids, there are shiny Instagram accounts and the idea that everyone who "does business" is supposed to be at least a millionaire. All you hear about are Mark Zuckerberg and Elon Musk, two billionaires in jeans and t-shirts. "Great, I want that, too!" But, in addition to everything that these boys have done brilliantly and correctly, there is one thing above all that they have achieved—one thing that you don't read about in the newspaper, and that you don't necessarily understand when you are looking at them. The special ingredient, the secret sauce of every idea, every company, and every champion, is *leadership*. The leader leads the team to safety. Like the Neanderthal before, today's leader shows the way through the tangled forest.

"But how do I lead, and which way should I go, because I don't see any path around here?!" That's right, because it doesn't exist yet. So let me be your leader, and guide you through ten thoughts that will make you an unstoppable trailblazer. Then you, too, can gather up and lead the next great leaders. Like a sharp machete, you will be able to cut your way through the densest jungle. You will be able to easily lead an army behind you that will fight with you in every battle. Not because you have lured them with filters, followers, and likes, but because you inspire. Trust earned through inspiration is the greatest gift, and the most rewarding respect anyone can ever give to you in the field of business. Come with me through these ten magical leadership lessons, and together let's venture our way to the highest levels of next-generation leadership. Follow me!

1. T-0-D-A-Y A LEADER

If you are a real world-class leader, it's never about problems becoming easier; it's all about you becoming better!

Here are five building blocks for the world-class leader in you, so that when you face the next difficult situation, you no longer have to ask yourself, "Why can't this be better, easier, more relaxed?" Instead, you'll ask yourself, "What can I do?" And not yesterday, not tomorrow, but instead—TODAY!

Total Devotion

The other day, I was in a really stupid situation. I was really pressed for time, and in my hurry, I badly scratched my car. Super annoying. So, I took it to a garage in Cologne, where I live. The shop is run by two older German men, but they are never there. The real heart of the shop is an Italian mechanic named Nino, who appears to be in his late thirties. A single father of a little boy, Nino speaks with an Italian accent about his love of cars. A really good guy.

So I dropped off my car at this small but cozy workshop that Nino usually runs all by himself. On the wall is a poster of an old Fiat 500, and another of winding Roman alleys in the summer, with the laundry hanging out of the windows, and flowers in bloom. When you look at these posters, you can almost smell the flowers and the fresh laundry. There's Italian music on the radio, and Nino is great to deal with. Typically, he springs out from beneath a car, and greets me warmly. "Ah, Matteo!" (Like all the Italians in my life, he doesn't call me Matthew.) "Ciao, bello! What have you done to your car this time? Such a deep scratch! You really put some effort into this one!" And when I entrusted my car to him, I already had a good feeling. It was like dropping off my little brother in kindergarten—no worries at all. "Don't worry, Matteo," Nino said. "I'll take care of everything!"

Two days later, I walk into the lot to pick up my car, and I can hardly believe my eyes: Not only is the scratch gone, but the sun is reflected in the perfectly polished paint, everything inside is clean and vacuumed, the car smells like new, and the rims are perfectly polished. Everything is sparkling.

And Nino gives me the keys as if he wants to hand me a present. "Isn't she beautiful?" he says quietly.

I can hardly answer. "Unbelievable, Nino! Awesome! All I wanted was that scratch repaired!"

Nino looks deep into my eyes, and says calmly, "Matteo, you don't understand. I love cars! I love my job! I can't think of anything better than being here with the cars every day. It makes me so happy to treat each car as if it's the last one I'll ever be allowed to work on. I'm really happy when the customers pick up their car, more beautiful than ever before, and I see that they are happy. This is my life, Matteo!"

That is total devotion.

Nobody watched him polish my car for hours, even though I only wanted a small scratch repaired. Nobody praised him. He does it because it's the right thing to do—today! Don't do what's easy, do what's right!

Michael Jordan, the basketball legend and one of my favorite athletes, once said, "How hard do you train when nobody is watching?" This question requires true leadership. Because what do the majority of people do? Everybody looks busy as soon as the boss comes in. When the boss goes out, everyone slacks off again. Classic.

Now back to you. Be honest: How hard do you push it if no one is watching, and when nobody needs to be impressed? What about when you're still sitting at your desk at night? Doing what's right, not what's easy—that's what this is about. For you and for your pride! You make yourself happy and proud because you know what's right. That goes for everyone. No matter who you are, you should be a leader. Whether a boss or an employee like Nino, you are a leader, and can do the right thing, not the easy thing. It's your decision!

So when it gets difficult, first ask yourself: What can I do? Not yesterday, not tomorrow, but today. "Where is my total devotion?"

"HOW HARD DO YOU TRAIN WHEN NOBODY'S WATCHING?"

—MICHAEL JORDAN

For the skeptics who are thinking, "Nice story, Matthew. I wish I had someone like Nino in my shop, because I have to correct my employees ten times before they get things right!" So here's an important idea: the behavior that's rewarded is the behavior that's repeated. So if somebody does something great, go crazy with praise and joy! And I swear to you, it will happen again. It's not so much about repeatedly micromanaging and correcting the wrong approach, but rather about celebrating the right approach. Establish a culture of being joyful when the right things happen, and people will show real dedication!

Again, for the skeptics, "But my employees don't want to celebrate. They'd much rather get in quickly and get out quickly, without having to make social contact." This is due to an emotion that infects even the best teams like a virus: fear. Your team members put on a mask as protection. They're afraid. Afraid of being themselves. Afraid of not fitting in. Afraid of not doing enough. Afraid of looking weak. They hide in their everyday lives. They put on a costume. They dress up, leave their house, but leave their true self at home. Outside, they become someone else. The funny thing is that if you do experience them at home after work—with their kids and spouses—they are often completely different people. They laugh loudly; they are happy and totally open.

That's too bad, because people tend to think, "It's possible to be casual with them at home, but to be a real leader at work, I have to talk differently, stand and behave differently, and look differently— strong and tough. Only then will I be respected." The truth is that you only really connect with your team, your customers, and your fellow human beings when you are real. When you are yourself. When the leader takes the mask off, everyone on the team takes their masks off. Then things will be as magical as it is with a world champion soccer team. Guaranteed!

Do the right thing. Let's consider any winning team. The teammates know each other inside and out. They shower together, share hotel rooms, and train together every day. These guys are real with each other! No masks. What happens when someone does the right thing in such a team? What happens when the winning point is scored? Fake smiles and weird small-talk? Nope! They scream, hug each other, tear off their jerseys, dance and cry with of joy. That's where the deep connection and the win come from! No masks!

That is real. That's why it works. And that leads to the next system: emotion.

OPEN EMOTION

Be vulnerable! Laugh, cry, show real emotions, and your team will love you for it. Before they trust you, people want to know who you really are—behind the business, under the suit. It's not weak to show emotion; it shows character because it takes real courage! Anyone can show up and pretend to be the tough guy. Mask on, costume on, and the Halloween macho show begins, with everyone playing a role. But what works better, is when the leader comes in and shows emotion. "People, I'm scared, and don't know what to do. I need your help! Let's solve this problem together. We can do it!"

Those are the words of a real leader. Strong leaders, through their emotional honesty, serve as role models to inspire and motivate people to become better.

Another aspect of emotion is getting to know each other! Really. No small talk. Look into each other's eyes, and really speak with interest about the other person's emotions. And I'm talking about both the team and the customer. Talk to the customers. When is their birthday? What are their problems? Remember their names and the names of their kids. I travel a lot. If I ever go to a place twice, and revisit a restaurant or hotel, it's usually for one reason. Because the owner knows my name, or the staff was really friendly. It's that simple!

Here's a practical "take-home tip": Buy a postcard! Send this postcard to the next customer who places an order with you. Simply write on it "Thank you for your trust!"

Difference

Say "thank you" more often; it costs nothing and can do anything. Be the nicest person you know and everything will change, immediately. It's not just the words "thank you." It's about the basics. Only if the basics are done right can the rest work. Only if the foundation is stable will the house survive the storm.

A few years ago, my uncle died. Much too early, God bless him. It was really sad. But it was incredibly beautiful that a couple hundred people attended his funeral. My uncle was not a politician, not a star. He was a normal man, with a normal job, but he really understood the basics! He was always happy and positive, always had a smile on his face. Always helped when he could. He had really good manners. He always thought of others before he thought of himself. He truly loved his wife of forty years. Never wanted to impress anyone; never wanted to be the very best. He led a very humble, simple life, was modest, and never materialistic. He didn't make millions, didn't build big companies. Like a small child, he could enjoy the little things in life.

A pure heart, a faithful soul, a great friend, and a really good uncle. He was a magician, and I will never forget how he showed new tricks to us children. For me, his magic was always real! My uncle was just a really good man. He understood the basics, and so touched hundreds of people in his short life—people who, even after his death, wanted to say goodbye to him. Learn to understand the basics, and you'll have a foundation on which to build a great life!

Another way to make a small difference: amaze your customers by under-promising and over-delivering! I learned this wisdom from my really cool operational management professor from the United States, Dr. Bruce Kibler, who had many years of management experience with major global players. At the time, I was maybe twenty years old, and it was the first semester of my business studies. I had no clue about anything and was sitting somewhere in the far back of the lecture hall, when I heard Dr. Kibler say this magical sentence: "Guys, remember this: Always under-promise and over-deliver!" From then on, I was hooked!

From that moment on, he had me. And even today, in the consulting or speaking work I do—with big companies, heavy hitters—I still share that phrase because it's so simple and so effective. Don't say, "Yes, it'll be ready tomorrow," only to find you have to push hard and hand over some half-finished thing. No! Say, "It'll be ready Saturday!"—and then on Thursday hand off a perfectly done project that no one expected so soon. It builds trust. That's what it's all about. Under-promise, over-deliver! Thanks, Dr. Kibler!

One last thought about the important difference: touch people's hearts! Every day, I deal with hard values, cash, strategy, rationalism. There actually are more important things than these—and now we're skating on thin ice. "Cash is king," is what I hear again and again. "Touch hearts, Matthew? Honestly! That's so bland, so kitschy." But consider this—the competition is everywhere, and it is really hungry! Here's an example: I'm looking for something on the Internet, and immediately the whole world wants to sell me that something! And at great prices. This is how Google display ads work.

The ads follow me ten pages further, and a pop-up offers me every kind of extra: free shipping, express shipping, 20 percent off, and everything else it can throw in as a bonus. But right now, I'm only buying the cheapest. My decision is purely price-driven. People want to pay the cheapest price, period. Huge deals require low prices. You can't win that battle if you don't scale like the big players, because today the margins are tiny. But if you touch their hearts, you don't get just the customer (for which you have to fight the whole world), you also get loyalty. You get an evangelist, a real fan who talks about you and creates virality! Are you telling anyone about the six-pack of AAA batteries you got at such a great discount on the internet? No, because it was only about the price. But Nino, the auto mechanic who touched my heart with his true devotion and became part of this book—I'm telling people about him, I'm doing his marketing for him! Do you understand what I mean? Touch hearts and you win real fans!

ALL-STAR TEAMWORK

Leadership is teamwork, and it's about people. Business is like a conversation, a constant dialogue with your team, with your customers, and with yourself. When was the last time you really spoke to your team about things that have nothing to do with work? When was the last time all of you looked each other in the eye and asked, "How are you, really?" Thanks to social networks, it takes one second to send a message to our buddy across the globe. Free of charge, immediately. How often do we use this extraordinary technology to create good relationships? And when it comes to the real world, we often don't take even two steps across the hallway to introduce ourselves to our neighbors. Doing everything is now possible using only SMS, email, or telephone, although the latter is already extinct (or at least critically endangered). Let me ask another question. When was the last time you wrote someone an SMS with the words,

"Can I call you right now?"

Yup, it's probably been a while, even though a phone call is far more personal than words on a screen.

Teamwork is about real human connections. Trust, loyalty, honesty. Eating together, sharing things, and really getting to know people. And what starts with the team, ends with the customer. If you build teams that allow for humanity and vulnerability, teams that help each other, where the weaker is given a helping hand upwards, then those same values are passed on to the customer. In a culture where people are proud of their work, and are allowed to make mistakes and grow, teams win together!

I'm always asked, "Are human connections what this is really about? Does it really work if I lead my team in a loose manner? Don't I have to be tough? Don't I have to be strict?" And I never answer with a monologue about leadership styles. (Anyway, monologues are obsolete if we decide to be real, rather than rattle on following a script.) Instead, I answer with the quote from Gandhi, "Be the change that you wish to see in the world!" Do you want a team whose members support each other? Then support your team! Do you want a team whose members deal openly with each other? Then deal openly with your team. But you have to be an example!

YOUR DECISION

The decision is the foundation stone, and the one that also closes the circle so that now everything makes sense! The decision to start, the decision to take the first step—a single right decision has the power to change your whole life!

For those who have difficulty making really good decisions, here are three key points for maximum decision-making power, and for a true doer mentality.

FIRST KEY POINT

Keep your eyes on the road! Especially if you are successful! I often present to really smart folks, successful people who are really cleaning up. They think, "It's going well with me, what do you have to teach me?" Exactly this: If it's working out, and it's going right, that's exactly when it becomes dangerous. When you're flying along at 160 miles per hour on the success highway of your life, then you tend to stop concentrating on the road.

You're having a conversation, everything's great. You are looking out the window on the left, looking out the window on the right, but forgetting the customer, and forgetting how careful you were in the early days. And then, all of a sudden, there's a bang, and nobody saw it coming. "But everything was going so well!" How many times have I heard that sentence! If you're really successful, it becomes really dangerous. Success, money, and power often correlate with arrogance, laziness, and complacency. So keep your eyes on the road, especially when things suddenly start going fast!

"BE THE CHANGE YOU WISH TO SEE IN THE WORLD!"

—MAHATMA GANDHI

SECOND KEY POINT
Do what you don't want to do first!

First thing in the morning, tackle the thing that's bothering
you most; make the phone call that you're least up for.
Why? Because you'll feel really good afterwards, and
because you make the best decisions in the morning (see
Willpower Muscle)!

Here is my advice: take risks, stand out in the big meeting,
and go straight for the difficult customer! Your personal
growth comes to fetch you, cloaked as fear. When things
get hard, you grow. When companies invite me to speak, to
advise them, to restructure things, to change processes,
and to make suggestions, I always remind everyone right
at the start that the change itself—which is sometimes
difficult and strange—is the first sign of success. The
unpleasant feeling at the start of a new change is the
first harbinger of growth. It becomes immediately clear:
something is happening, and you can feel it. That distinct
feeling is all I care about. Learning and growing.

Living your best life is all about evolving—every day, today.
All the things that happen to you, good and bad, are part of
your growth education, and you must use them.

THIRD KEY POINT
One-inch victories! It's not always about the big things,
but about continual small victories, every day. That's what
it's about. I call them the "'one-inch victories.'" Not much,
I know, but what do you have after a month of continuous
one-inch victories? Thirty-one inches. After a year? More
than ten yards. Everyday, small victories add up to big
successes. It's not about the end result—it's about the
person you become with every new day and with every new
inch. One inch per day, and you'll actually advance by yards.
Guaranteed! That applies to everything: learning, health,
creativity, fitness, business, family, and relationships.

One inch alone is not much, but it always makes a difference. Have you ever seen a photo finish horse race? Fractions of an inch can decide the big victory. The gymnastics world champion Fabian Hambüchen once told me that he often only discovers mistakes in his maneuvers on the high bar when he analyzes the videos: "We work with angle measurements and millimeter-precise observations. Sometimes, it's just a few millimeters that prevent you from sticking the landing!" It's exactly the same in life. Sometimes it's so little, and yet so much, that decides everything in the end. The one inch is decisive at the end, but it's also especially so at the start. Your first inch is the most important! Every professional was once a beginner. Every master was a disaster. But inch by inch, day by day, you move forward. Don't stop. Keep growing. There's no goal, just your path—One inch per day!

This rule applies to everyone, because we're all the same. We all have twenty-four hours in a day. And yet we keep pointing out people and saying, "Wow! Somehow, they're special!" Mark Zuckerberg, Bill Gates, Cristiano Ronaldo, and other big names like them. No, they're human, too! The only difference is they made a decision, they started, they've grown one inch every day, always moving forward, day by day. They have always believed that in the end, everything will work out, that the path is the victory, that every day counts, and that every mistake is valuable! The big, successful players are no different than you and me, but possibly they made a lot more mistakes. If you don't make enough mistakes, you're not trying hard enough! Those who don't make a lot of mistakes aren't reaching for the highest goal. So, reach for the stars, and fall down often. And start today!

No matter what it is—it can be a very small thing—start it today! Give a nice smile to a stranger. Start that project you've been postponing for so long. Start going to the gym. Say hello to the nice girl or guy you that you have always passed by and then got mad at yourself for not saying anything. Go the first inch today. Tell your family today how much you love them. I read again and again that older people who are dying all say the same thing: "I wish I'd dared more, laughed more, told my loved ones more often how much I love them, overcome my fears, and lived my dreams." It's the things you don't do and the opportunities you don't use that at some point will tear you apart.

Live as if it were your last day? No. We've definitely heard that saying too often! Live as if it were the last day for every other person in the world. You will never see them again, but you will remember forever everything you could have done but didn't. Now, take out your cell phone or laptop (or a card and pen), and write to someone you appreciate, and to whom you rarely say that. No long explanation, no long story, just a few nice words. Not because you want to get something back, but because you want to give something.

Do today the things that you'll thank yourself for tomorrow.

2. WHAT YOU CAN LEARN FROM CHILDREN

Let's think for a moment about really awesome leaders. Who comes to mind? Are they business celebrities, football gods, war heroes, or politicians? But this section is not about the classic superstars, but about real, authentic leaders, about big and fearless hearts, and about big visionaries, full of joy and happiness. Actually, I'm talking about children. Children are the best examples of world-class leadership! Children teach us again and again how life really functions. Children embody the key skills of true, great leaders, in a playful way, every day!

Check it out…

CHILDREN ARE CURIOUS!

Have you ever seen a kid who can't wait to open his Christmas present? It's a state of emergency. Pure curiosity. Really.

CHILDREN LOVE TO LEARN!

Are you familiar with those interactive audio learning books where if you press an apple icon the book loudly and irritatingly says *A—an apple*. After the first sound, you want to throw it out the iPad, but a child will play and learn with it for hours. Voluntarily.

CHILDREN ARE NOT AFRAID OF CHANGE!

Leave five kids who don't know each other in a sandbox, come back fifteen minutes later and you've got a really good party going on, with five new best friends. All shoes and trouser pockets full of sand. But put five adults in an elevator, and you get the following scene: dead silence, but everyone is pissed off because someone farted.

CHILDREN ALWAYS STAND UP AGAIN!

Before they can walk, every child has to fall and stand up again a thousand times. A child never gives up until they get it. I'm talking here about physically falling into the dirt, and then getting back up, a thousand times. This isn't about how a customer says "No" twice on the phone, and it feels like your whole day is now fucked. Falling down, on the floor, entire body flat on the stomach, and then up again, a thousand times. Until they get it. These are children.

Children try things out, and don't pay attention to what they look like to others! As a child, did you dance as if nobody was watching? I don't know what you looked like back then; I had some really questionable moves. But it was always fun! And nowadays? Have you gone dancing at a club lately? Really dancing, without paying attention to what others see—your hairstyle, clothes, the size of the champagne bottle, and every step? There's nothing really genuine anymore. That's sad.

CHILDREN GIVE IT THEIR ALL TO ACHIEVE THEIR GOALS!

Have you ever watched a child who wants a toy launch into a temper tantrum with his mom? That child should win an Oscar for best performance. To get what they want, kids throw themselves on the floor, scream, beat their fists, kick, and give it their all. Now there's someone who really wants to close the deal—someone who really wants something, and who's willing to give everything to get it.

CHILDREN LOVE WITH THEIR WHOLE HEART!

Do you have a little daughter or son? If not, try hugging a niece or nephew, a cousin, or any other four- or five-year-old child. It's like a kung fu stranglehold. You have to free yourself from the little arms, as if from octopus tentacles.

This is a real hug, not a careful, embarrassing half-hearted thing. They're all in, baby: Children are on the go with all their heart. They give the best hugs in the world!

So what's the difference between children and adults? Are we so much smarter, better, more mature, and so on? Well, I see it as the other way around! Adults are often more like spoiled children who've forgotten their dreams and wishes. The childlike love, innocence, happiness, visions, the laughter and the lightness have simply disappeared over time, buried deep beneath the rules of adulthood. Like mantras, children are always hearing sentences like: "You can't do this!" "You mustn't do that!" "You want to become an astronaut? Tell that to your father. First get your high school diploma, and then we'll discuss it." Big dreams are squeezed through the tiny needle's eye of seemingly irrevocable social rules, and are reduced to the safe, boring Chris Normal version. It's safer to do what everyone else does. Bullshit! Because when you're competing against the whole world, it's safer to do what no one else is doing.

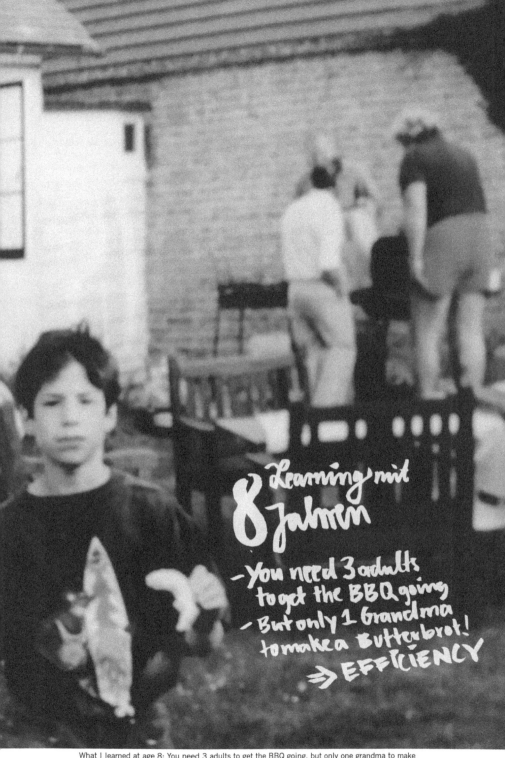

8 Learning mit Jahren

- You need 3 adults to get the BBQ going
- But only 1 Grandma to make a Butterbrot!
=> EFFICIENCY

What I learned at age 8: You need 3 adults to get the BBQ going, but only one grandma to make you a slice of butter bread. >>Efficiency

Ask a group of kindergarteners who of them can sing. All their hands go up. Ask this fifteen years later in a high school class. No one! Children think they are superheroes, and that's a good thing! Science has proven that this seemingly crazy imagination is directly linked to happiness, joy, and fulfillment.

In her book *SuperBetter*, Jane McGonigal talks about maximizing potential by living life playfully. What would you like to be able to do? In what do you need to become stronger? These questions will lead you to your superhero alter ego! Which superhero are you? I'd like to be "Matthew, the Event Slayer," who sells out every show with his four-person team of Entrepreneur Super Heroes.

How do you get there?

Through clear tasks that are set and solved every day. Everyday tasks that are suddenly brought to life. The office becomes a playing field; the routine becomes an exciting game. Give yourself extra points for tough boss moments, difficult phone calls, and long evenings. Reward yourself. Become the video game designer of your own world. Setting tasks for yourself creates perspective and responsibility, meaning and motivation. Accomplishing them makes you happy. Maximizing the dopamine release by reaching the next level is what keeps you in the game. You spend the best hours of your best life playing.

It's such a paradox that each year children grow bigger and bigger physically, but get smaller and smaller psychologically. In these key years of our development, physical size seems to correlate with mental regression—not intellectually, but spiritually. Our dreams, our ideas, our laughter, our imagination, our singing, our dance, and our love for life—all this gets smaller and quieter, and at some point almost disappears.

So, the crucial question: What must we do to reawaken the child in us? What must we do to unearth these childlike, world-class leadership skills that must be sleeping somewhere inside us, and bring them out into our best life? Maybe we'll just look exactly where the answer has always been. We'll ask someone who knows you inside and out, and who will never forget your greatest dreams and wishes: your eight-year-old self.

What would your eight-year-old self tell you about the person you are today? What would your eight-year-old self be proud of? To him or her, what about you today would be cool, what would be impressive, what would be a pity? Put this book aside for a moment and imagine this dialogue. Speak thoughtfully with this child about yourself, the person this child became. What are your current values, your principles? What do you stand for, and what are your goals?

The child in you knows the correct answers, knows what's right and what's wrong. They dream huge dreams and think nothing is impossible. Keep reconnecting with this child in you, and never forget that the child in you can fly through life with fearless ease. Every day, you have an opportunity to consciously listen to the child within you, to live the way you used to. Make it your goal every day to liberate a little more of the child in you, and do so until your inner child is very close to you again—full of joy and energy. You have the power to give the happiness of a child to each new day.

I'd like to tell a story about the days in your best life. A story that the child in you would enjoy. This story is about a photo wall—a wall filled from floor to ceiling with small photos. This photo wall belongs to you alone, because you yourself created every photo. Each picture represents one day in your life.

Imagine that you are now slowly walking along your very own photo wall and are taking a close look at every picture. With peace and with time, you study the individual days of your life. And now, ask yourself honestly and clearly: What have you experienced? Where are all the places you have been, and with whom, and what have you felt and why? What do you look like in those photos? Are you happy? Are you healthy? Are you fulfilled? Do your eyes laugh? Is your heart laughing? Are you living your authentic, best life in every single photo?

And suddenly, you come to a place where the pictures end abruptly. The last photo of you on your very own photo wall is a shot taken yesterday. After that, the wall is empty, naked, white, and untouched.

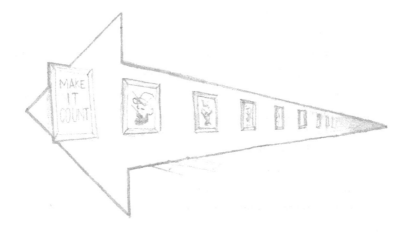

Starting today, you can consciously create each additional photo yourself. From the bottom of my heart, and full of respect and esteem for you and your decisions, I ask you to now promise yourself, and the child in you, to fill each new day with moments that make you happy and proud, days that are real and important, that fill you and let you grow, that are authentic and powerful. Live happy days, and create photos in which you are happy, in which you are living your best life—with all your heart, from within, fearless and pure, as you used to do as a child. Because there comes a day, I promise, when you are too old and too weak to walk up and down your photo wall. But your children, your grandchildren, great-grandchildren, and their children and grandchildren will be curious, and will love to look closely at every single picture on your photo wall. So make sure that every single picture, every day, makes you and everyone around you truly happy and proud.

WHAT DO YOU WANT TO LEAVE BEHIND?

Like every photo wall, yours will end sometime. Now, while you still have the ability to influence it, take the time and use your imagination to connect with your finiteness, just as you can connect with the child within you. Write your own obituary. What should people remember in your life when they think of you and talk about you? Sit and write down what you stood for, write down what distinguished you; make clear to yourself what made you special, and why the people who know you will miss you so much. What are you going to leave behind? Connect with your finiteness, and find out!

Far too often, people live as if their time on earth is infinite. They procrastinate: I'll start reading that new book tomorrow; I'll sign up for the gym next week; I'll start studying next year; I'll stop smoking next month; I'll start my diet again on Monday because now it's the weekend! People are masters of procrastination. But who knows how much time you have left in this world? Who knows if next week will be too late? Live your life in mini-wins. Create days during which you pay full attention, days whose potential you fully exploit for yourself and for your growth, for your development and for your greatest happiness! On their deathbeds, people mostly regret the things they didn't do. (If you still haven't written a quick note to your loved ones, just pop back to the "one-inch victories" section.) But we also keep postponing the moments of joy: "When I have a big car, when the sun is shining again, when the holidays start, and when I get the next big pay raise, then I'll be happy!" Big mistake. Right now is the only moment that you can actually control and consciously live and experience, that you can use for yourself and your best life. What happened five seconds ago is over, and what will happen in five seconds is something you don't know, but the moment in this second belongs to you alone, and it is perfect. Connect with the child in you, connect with the years of your youth, connect with your great desire for adventure, and live in the moment! Get out of your head, and into your heart! Feel life in this second, and enjoy the gift of these moments: they belong to you, and you can use them to grow. Congratulations! And thank you so much for sharing this precious moment with me.

3. LET'S TALK, BUT REALLY! HOW TO MASTER DIFFICULT CONVERSATIONS

Every interaction during your life will always involve some kind of conversation. Sometimes it'll be non-verbally—via a look, a feeling, or a hand signal—but you will be sending out information and emotions, and you will be expecting a response. Sounds easy, but what if things get difficult? What happens if a conversation doesn't work out the way you imagined? You know the moment well: the mood changes, each looks away. It's as if a horrible thunderstorm has suddenly gathered over your heads. It sets off the alarms. What's going on, and why is this happening?

But above all, how can we restore the sunshine as quickly as possible, without being unfaithful to our own position?

Let's start at the beginning. Let's clarify some vocabulary and be clear about their definitions. The moment it becomes awkward is usually when your conversation becomes really important! It's no longer about small talk. Suddenly, it's about everything, and the situation becomes "intense." The typical topics of intense conversations include relationships (love and/or friendship, family), money, working hours (and other variables in a business relationship), and any kind of criticism. If your conversation moves toward one of those topics, you'll immediately notice: Now it's getting intense! At that point, the biggest problem is that the conversation loses its looseness, and, figuratively speaking, both parties begin to "tug." It's no longer a matter of letting the stream of information flow into a common sea of knowledge, but now it's about right and wrong, winners and losers, scoring points at any price—often by using sarcasm, pressure, high volume, or negative silence. The "modern" human—a Neanderthal man in jeans and sneakers—recalls his time fighting mammoths, and changes from "conversational" to "survival mode." It becomes all about fight or flight.

Biologically, this is what happens: To make us fit for the upcoming fight, powerful adrenaline is pumped into the body directly from the adrenal glands. The important tools, the arms and legs—*yes, exactly, for kicking and punching*—are supplied with blood, and the whole body becomes tense. (I told you, the situation itself is tense!) We're now ready to face this intense conversation and either fight to the death (as we once did with the mammoth) or flee back to our cave. But what always worked well against the mammoth is counterproductive in our intense conversation today. It started out as a very important conversation (see above: family, money, friendship, job, etc.), but now we're ready to swing our club, although we would rather be mentally and physically preparing for an intellectual and empathic display of rhetoric and of cunning eloquence that would result in a gallant win-win situation.

So here's your game plan for when things start to get shaky. You'll notice that a thunderstorm is coming; no question about it, it's soon going to get intense. But before you fall back into battle position, fearing for your survival, you will ask yourself a few complex questions, so that your blood will have to travel to your brain instead of to your armory. Ask yourself questions that will summon the juicy and truly useful material that you will need for great dialogues and for compromises.

THE 4-STEP PROCESS

Remember, there will be no winner and no loser in your next intense conversation, only a win-win situation. Here are the questions to ask yourself:

1

PUSH THROUGH
"HOW DO WE STAY IN THE CONVERSATION?"

What's the best thing you could do to push through this intense conversation? Your willingness to push through—come what may— creates trust and genuine respect. Here, two parties face each other, and make it clear right from the start, "We're not leaving the table until we're both happy!" Sentences like "It's really important to me that we leave with a good feeling and find a solution that we both really like" create great starting points. Let's keep going!

2

REASON
"WHAT DOES MY CONVERSATION PARTNER (REALLY) WANT?"

What is the reason for their position? To find out exactly what your conversation partner wants, just ask them. "I'd like you to help me to understand your point of view as well as possible so I can continue with relevant information. Tell me, what exactly do you want and why?" An honest interest in their wishes creates the basis for a good, open conversation. You ask for help (opening yourself physically and emotionally), put your partner in a strong position, and show empathy. Now listen carefully to what they tell you, because their reason and strategy are often completely different. A disagreement is usually much easier to resolve through reasoning than by letting the disagreement escalate. Would you like an example?

Alright. You're the boss, and you're inviting folks to a company outing. One of your board members cancels unexpectedly, and you're disappointed. In most cases, the communication stops here. We have a classic case of non-verbal communication that ends with a strong emotional impact. You didn't even look each other in the eye, and yet you are disappointed, and your board member, who had to cancel, is certainly not unaffected either.

As an honest boss and good communicator, you seek an open dialogue to try to find out the reason behind the cancellation and whether or not the situation can be salvaged. You call, "Hey, I heard you cancelled the trip. You know how much I like and respect you, and how much I would have loved to have you join me. I don't want to pressure you, but please help me understand why you cancelled." The other person feels secure and comfortable in this dialogue, and what could have been a rather intense conversation (they could have assumed that you were angry, disappointed, and hurt) now becomes very relaxed; there's no tension. In this setting, your conversation partner can open up and tell you that a family event had been scheduled for Sunday, the second day of the company trip. It becomes clear how important this event is to him, even though, as a board member, the company is (of course) another clear priority.

We see a classic case of being torn between two choices, but no worries. So far, so good!

3

MISSION
"WHAT WOULD OUR COMMON GOAL LOOK LIKE?"

Do we have a common mission? As soon as we can agree on a common mission, the dangerous tension transforms into a common movement forward. We're now transferring all the power of the situational emotion into a shared conviction and synergy.

Let's stick with our example. "I think it's really great how important your family is to you, and that you don't want to cancel your Sunday plans with your loved ones. I completely understand that, and I'd do the same. I'm glad to support you, not only as a business partner, but also as a person. At the same time, I'd like to discuss our common mission and conviction with you. Is it true that we both wish for a healthy and fulfilling life with our families, and a successful cooperation in this company, which feeds our families and enables them—and us—to do so much?" Thus, we converge on a common denominator: our mission, the conviction to combine family happiness and business. This synergy makes us a single person for a moment. Tension becomes lightness; the tug-of-war becomes a common thrust.

IMPLEMENTATION
"HOW DO WE ACHIEVE OUR COMMON GOAL?"
What would the solution look like?

The solution is practically obvious. Without pressure, the solution came about simply by having the right questions, a healthy mood, and real synergy. Your partner is now able to express what you yourself are thinking; now you're both on the same wavelength. "Thank you very much for this nice conversation and for your understanding! I'd like to be there on Saturday, the first day of the trip. And I'll spend Sunday with my family, if that's alright." A flawless win-win situation has been created, without tension and pressure, without winners and losers, points, clubs, mammoths, fights, or anything else.

In your next intense conversation, stand mentally beside your counterpart, not in front of them or even above them. You're running a marathon together, so keep each other in the race if you want to finish together. Every victory, especially a win-win, is always the result of a team that plays together!

Intense conversations are only as productive as their protagonists. Make sure that both of you leave an intense conversation as winners and with the understanding that you can only win this victory together. Only as a team can you bring sunshine into a thunderstorm, can you surf the waves of your win-win sea, and draw new energy from synergy. The fight for survival must become a fight for the common goal.

4. A 10 OVER YOUR HEAD

Some people always make talking to others look so easy. Do you know folks like that? They walk into a room and—boom! They have everyone's attention—in a good way. And you see it happen, and you sense that it works. And you wonder "How do they do that?"

I like to imagine a number that floats above your head. Every person gets a number from 1 to 10. "1" means "I'm not interested at all." "10" means "Wow, whoever this is, I have to get to know them!" Have you ever seen a "10"? They come into the room, and it's immediately clear that something's going on. The air sizzles. Some people call it an aura, others call it sex appeal, and others just say "They've really got something!" And I'm telling you, they do have something, a "10" over their head. What's interesting is the possibility that this number used to be a 3, but through continued education, and through work on self-confidence, body language, and personality development, it eventually became a 10. Nobody's born with a 10 over his head; it comes from training—like developing a "six pack." One thing's clear: you have to hit the gym in the winter so that everything looks reasonable on the beach in the summer.

Let's keep this short. No matter what's above your head, you can turn it into a 10. I'm not just saying maybe, but for sure—100 percent.

FOUR THOUGHTS TO INCREASE YOUR SCORE

Here are four thoughts that can in the next five minutes raise the number above your head by up to three points.

1. EYE CONTACT

Please, not a sick Robocop "laser look." But nice! Your glances connect and register. Okay, everything feels cool and nice, and now we can get closer! Not so different from flirting. A confident look in your eyes is genuine and courageous, showing interest, openness, respect. It's those things that always get under someone's skin.

We've lost our ability to look outwards. Artificially illuminated screens, mobile phones, laptops, TV—everything happens about fifteen inches away from our eyes. Our visuality is forced to regress. Look into the distance; look into the eyes of strangers. Look beyond your personal horizon. There's a saying, "The eyes are the windows to the soul!" It's a very powerful tool, this deep look into someone's eyes, or the long view into the distance.

2. BODY POSTURE

Imagine that you're a puppet with strings on all its limbs. Okay, now *also* be the puppeteer. Use the strings on your head, shoulders, and elbows to stand up straight, confident, and with good posture. This is very important not only visually, but also mentally. A stooped posture always means a stooped soul. Have you ever observed someone who's really happy? They stand proud. And you can use this technique to give yourself a similar mindset—without winning the lottery, just with your posture. Modern technology leads more and more to the breakdown of human physiology, posture, and physicality. We lean over the phone, the laptop. In nature, this is a posture of fear and submissiveness: shoulders hanging, back bent, arms crossed. It's as if our being is physically closing off, for protection. This physiological posture psychologically influences us, weakening us from the outside to the inside and vice versa—a negative feedback loop. Stand straight, feel those strings, feel the excitement! And immediately, you'll feel strong, well, and secure.

3. THE FIRM HANDSHAKE

Call me old-fashioned, but a firm handshake is incredibly important. Have you ever met someone who offered you a dead fish handshake? One that's still dripping wet? It's terrible! People, our bodies are meeting for the first time. What do you want to communicate with your handshake? Of course, self-confidence, poise, pride, and transparency. Joy, but also serenity. Strength, but also security. With this gesture, peace is made, wars are ended, and billions of deals are concluded. When I have a daughter, it's obvious that the handshake of her first boyfriend will be an absolute knock-out criterion, a life-or-death decision-maker.

A good handshake is so crucial. Straight ahead, short, firm, and good. Don't try anything crazy, don't do too much! Not this sideways twister. Do you know what I mean? Oh man, like a kung fu fighter! And please don't double-up. You know the two-hander? When the left hand is put on top of the other two hands, as if the Pope is greeting you? Don't ever do this! And be careful to avoid the too-cool handshake—such as a slick "Fresh Prince of Bel-Air" right-left combination. No! And please, no dead fish! Nor that loose, barely-there, let's-see-what-happens grip.

Straight, short, firm, good—boom!

4. WORD CHOICE

Have at least one good sentence ready—always! Both for the intro and for the outro. There's nothing worse than going in and not knowing what you want to say! Not "Well, my name's Matthew. I'm here just like you are. Well, nice weather, huh?" Screw that, dude! The number over your head just went to negative 20. Nor "Yeah, well, I'm gonna go now." Or even worse, the "sneak away"—just wordlessly and slowly moving away. That doesn't work at all.

Have something ready—always—and have at least two sentences per situation! It's always the same, anyway. You could arrive at night and wake me up, but boom, I say "Hey, my name is Matthew Mockridge. I'm so happy!" Then the reply is always, "Hey, I'm happy, too. My name is Peter Lustig!" (Okay, *of course* the name changes each time!) After that, you need to follow up with something purposeful—and immediately—because otherwise it will be embarrassing. Next sentence: "Peter, really glad to meet you, do you have a card?" Starting today, always ask for a card! Cards are like banknotes. We gladly accept them, but we don't like to give them. (No one has ever liked putting their card in other people's faces. In new situations we consciously stay about 10 percent below our normal energy level, that way we appear calm, modest, and relaxed.)

Here's a little tip: always put the accepted card in your right pocket, and always hand yours out of your left pocket, so nothing gets mixed up. Then ask a nice open question for Peter: "What brings you here?" Now, he can tell you something. (I call this "Small Talk Soccer," and I'm gonna make sure you become Small Talk Soccer Player of the Year!)

You respond to Peter by saying "Awesome. Very nice, Peter. Dreamy. I'm really jealous!" (By the way, you should only say that if the two of you are not kidding around!) See, you just let him win! Your intuition tells you that you yourself want to win Small Talk Soccer—using your cool step overs, hook moves, and corner kicks. But things are different here. Boys who want to win just talk about how great they are, what kind of cars they drive, how much money they earn—all corner kicks. But no one wants to hear that! So make Peter feel big, let him win, and he'll think, "Wow, what a great guy, and what a nice conversation!" Actually, that's your victory. Peter likes you. Congratulations! The seed is planted, and now it's time to go! You immediately recognize the moment when it gets awkward, and when the stoppage time has started running. At this point, don't be the kind who "sneaks away," but rather like a strong midfield play-maker. You take the ball, and run with it yourself, "Peter, I'm going to continue making the rounds for a little while, but I am really glad we met. And it's good that I have your card." (Remember, it's in your right pocket.) "I wish you a wonderful evening!"

A short, firm, good handshake—and you're out! It's a win-win!

The trick: "island hopping," a system that I developed for myself as a networking tool to connect at events as efficiently as possible. At NEON-SPLASH – Paint-Party®, I was responsible for business development (a fancy word for salesman).

I had to find partners, sponsors, licensees, and bookers. So, I'm standing around at all kinds of events, in VIP areas and at galas, and don't know a single soul. And I keep thinking to myself "I don't know anybody here, so how am I supposed to connect without coming across as strange? But who the hell is that guy over there who knows and is greeting everyone?" (Guys like that seem to be everywhere.) I was a bit sad, but I also had just made my most important observation—the person who seemed to know everyone.

Own the Whole Room in Ten Minutes

Now I'll tell you a party trick (in the truest sense of the word)! Ever been to a party where there's one guy who seems to know everybody? Well, this guy is usually me, but it's not because I know everyone, and it's not because I'm so popular or well-known or anything else. I know how to be that guy, even if I'm in a strange city and I don't know a single person. And now I'll show you how to master this game right away.

Eventually I began to really take the time to observe the interactions that this type of person had with other people, noticing their appearance, the intervals between greetings, the gestures, the postures, the reactions. And I did this in different cities, and with different versions of this type of person. Most of the time there was only a short wave or nod, a handshake and a few words. Not much, but effectively giving other people the impression that he knows everyone. This was a giant "aha!" moment for me! His status resides in social perception: everybody thinks he knows everyone, because it looks like he does. Okay, maybe Mr. Connected does actually know them, but that's irrelevant for the effect, the appearance. So, I figured out a system that would allow me to exactly mirror this effect and recreate the same result within a radius of ten to twenty feet, at every party, in every city. Here's how it works:

Just give out ten compliments! Make a round at the event you're at. Doesn't matter if it's a birthday, wedding, party, pub, conference, and so forth. Give a serious compliment to ten strangers during this round, and then ask for their names and introduce yourself. Something like, "Wow, cool sneakers! (Thank you.) My name is Matthew, nice to meet you. (Nice to meet you, too, my name's XY.) Alright, XY, see you later. Have fun!" After you've done this with ten different people in the room, you've created your islands. In theory, you could hardly go through the room without meeting one of your islands. Of course, you do it with great joy about the reunion, a handshake, a pat on the shoulder, and a "Hey, XY, are you having fun?"

You have created a base, and now you can move safely through people. You have anchor points, goals, and reasons to move. You've met at least ten people (by now that's become thirty to forty); you interact authentically and in a relaxed way. The most important thing is that everyone else is watching you (just like you've always watched that type of guy), and now they also want to get to know you (drum roll, please).

You have now, out of nowhere and in less than ten minutes, created a magnetic effect. Effectively, you have drawn to yourself some of the general interest of the people at this event. At this point, you can, if you like, introduce yourself (in a similar way) to anyone in the place, without it feeling strange (because you already know so many people here). Without problems, you can connect to anyone.

I once pulled this one off at an evening event at the electro-music festival ADE in Amsterdam—and I did it so excessively that in the end I said goodbye to about fifty people (whom I did not know before) with high-fives and hugs. I was there with a potential partner, who now of course wanted to work together with me, because the whole gang's interaction with me helped him decide. It's all about using the energy in the room. People always think the same thing in event settings: "Hopefully, everyone doesn't think I look lost!" Going up to someone (anyone!) who feels like that with a compliment, a smile, and a handshake is a win-win. It always works, building you your islands for the night of your life!

In case you found that tip helpful, here's a look at my networking trick kit.

A short disclaimer: I'm a fan of good conversations with depth and with serious common interest. At the same time, I always find myself in situations where it's difficult to have a "real" conversation (networking events, trade shows, conferences, seminars, gyms, supermarkets, etc.). The atmosphere is best-suited for the short exchange of words: intro, handshake, a few sentences—and then you (or your conversation partner) have to move on. For this type of stage and this short speaking role, the following mini-script should help. Our goal is to leave a good, confident, lasting impression. Not pushy, just honest and controlled. No fluff. But most importantly, even when it comes to small talk, our goal is a long-term connection. Real niceness, honest interest. Not a transaction, but an exchange.

To address the Big Points of your networking performance in as structured a way as possible, and to optimize them in detail, we will map your micro-interaction in three acts: Setting, Performance, and Exit. Like in a film.

SETTING

The setting determines the show and, therefore, should always be considered before the actual performance. How are the vibes? What energy is in the air? Who would you like to meet? How busy are these people? Evaluate the energy of your environment and let it help determine the intensity and attitude you will employ to face the audience! Just chill, breathe, detach from the crowd, and let your gaze glide over the people. Sense the right moment for your next move. Put yourself slightly below the energy level of the room—always a few percentage points below the norm. Not slow, not at low speed, but just a bit more relaxed than average. Your relaxed attitude helps make your counterparts feel comfortable. How well did the last conversation go when some nervous energy drink- or cocaine-fueled junkie drilled a pitch into your head that sounded like a double-speed track from Eminem? You don't conform to the room, but are a little calmer, a little looser, a little clearer, and a little cooler. That is the perfect state of mind before you step out "on stage."

A good tip for the Setting: Do a small warm-up. Prep yourself with a few sentences. Have some good, short mini-dialogues with people for whom you don't need a special intro, and who don't make you nervous (bar staff, admission staff, coat check, etc.)! Offer a few compliments, ask questions, and warm up! Each session of "small talk" will make you more self-confident and secure. Get into your flow. Feel good in this setting!

ALCOHOL

If alcohol is a part of the event (especially at the after parties and meetups), then always drink a glass of water between the alcoholic drinks. A rule of thumb: always one water for each drink. It's best to avoid shots altogether because of their high alcohol concentration. Otherwise, always favor clear alcohol over dark (these may contain acetone and acetaldehyde). Order lemons or limes at the bar and squeeze them into the water. Fructose helps to metabolize the alcohol, preventing a hangover.

PROSPECTING

We're still talking about the Setting. You should be clear about whom you would like to talk to. If it's a completely new setting (foreign industry, first visit to a trade fair, etc.), study in advance the partnerships, connections, and faces. The more fixed points you have, the shorter the lines between your fixed points, and the tighter your network. Remember that everyone wants to chat with the Big Guys, so find alternative entry points. No matter how great your idea is, for them, the 200th pitch of the day is always annoying. Try to identify a less frequented, less "guarded" entry point. Special Forces usually come through windows, the roof, or other "back doors," and not through the front door.

THREE "UNDER THE RADAR" ENTRY POINTS

WHAT IS YOUR BIG GUY READING?

Which books, blogs, and authors does your target read? (To find out, read interviews, and listen to them on podcasts.) If you can establish connections with those authors and hosts, you'll not just be seen by your target, but also gain credibility because someone they trust may be talking or writing about you. Let others make the pitch for you.

WHO'S IN THE ENTOURAGE?

At conferences, trade fairs or seminars, your target person's entourage stays behind them or within a twelve-foot radius: personal assistants, PR staff, managers, buddies, cofounders, and partners. The entourage is always happy to have nice conversations since (at least for a moment!) the attention is turned to them, as people. It's very important to remember that we are not using them as stepping stones, but that we are making nice, honest, emotional connections. Your motto is "be interested," not "be interesting." If you are interested and authentic, then the path into the entourage is not difficult. And once you are in the entourage, your path to the target person is much shorter. You might also learn something new!

WHO IS THE NEXT BIG GUY?

Instead of trying to run after the current Hot Shot, like everyone else is doing, you could simply project your input onto the future. Find out who's doing the next big thing, whose book is about to be released! The people in demand today were only insider tips yesterday. Find these people and build authentic win-win relationships with them! It's important to be nice to everyone because anyone could be the next industry superstar (including yourself). Niceness always promises to be long-term, especially since we are building the foundations for lifelong, real connections, not for some selfish business-oriented one-night stand.

If you want to know what your future looks like, look at your decisions today! Do something today that your future self will be grateful for. And if you want to know how your fellow human beings will treat you, look at how you treat them: karma!

YOUR PERFORMANCE

If you see someone you want to meet, don't think long about it. Just turn the situation around. Everyone is happy to be addressed nicely—that's human. So, ask yourself, "How would I like to be addressed?" And then do exactly that! Your speed and your own strong determination will help you over any initial difficulty. Allow yourself no more than three seconds to think about a speech. Start immediately! To overcome your reluctance, use the neurotransmitter dopamine, which is released in the prefrontal cortex of the brain. This short "high" carries you from the intro to the next part.

If you're still unsure, ask yourself, "What would I do if I were the hero in an action movie and a whole movie theater full of people was watching now?" This perspective opens up your imagination, your vision, and your ability to make great moves and give strong performances.

Visualize mastering a mission in a third-person shooter video game—your own *Grand Theft Auto*—so that you can move on to the next level. This technique is effective because in pressure situations people are very visual. Gymnasts and high jumpers, for example, always imagine their routines and rotations exactly before they do their routine. Everything you see in your mind becomes reality!

SOME TIPS FOR THE ICEBREAKER

In your perception, the first sentence is always the most difficult, so make it especially easy for yourself: no long intros, no memorized elevator pitches that no one wants to hear, but a short compliment. Nothing more. And nothing that makes you seem weird. Just be simple and clear, and always with a relaxed smile: "Cool shirt!" "I like your hat!" "Good speech!"

Statements that connect you with others also work well. Emotional connections always create a good basis for a conversation. "It's so hot in here!" "The parking situation was tricky." "The chicken skewers are awesome, aren't they?" Once there is an emotional connection, the follow-up must be a question the person hasn't heard—at worst—200 times earlier today. Questions like "What do you do?" are on the blacklist and should never be used. Ask strong questions that address the person—*not* their potential benefits. "Where are you from?" is great, and usually creates a solid basis for discussion, especially if you follow up with something like, "Ah, from Chicago. Okay. Also born there? No? What brought you to Seattle from Chicago?" And now you're talking about your jobs, backgrounds, and stories, letting your conversation become truly emotionally valuable.

Only a conversation that is emotionally valuable can also be commercially valuable. Why? Because business is done between people, and nobody wants to work with an asshole. One of our company principles is "We don't work with assholes!" That's how it is. And this brings us back to the fundamental point: be nice to everyone!

Icebreakers in one-on-one settings are always easier. For approaching a group, I've adhered to the following strategy (with it, I've had the most success). Basically, if it's a group of two, don't even bother. A group of three is okay, as long as you make a modest entrance.

The strongest intros are always the ones that immediately make it clear that you carry a white flag, and don't want anything bad. (Don't sell anything, don't pitch anyone, and don't pick up contacts.) This technique works especially well if for a moment you perform under your level of competence. Something like this:

"Hey, excuse me if I'm intruding. I'm here for the first time. I don't know anyone and wanted to ask if I could just listen to you. I'll buy a round of drinks if you want." That shouldn't be a problem most of the time. And at some point, the following will happen: someone in the group will ask what you do. Now comes the time to use a handy ultra-short version of your story. That means the part of your story that they can really appreciate because it shows an intersection between you. What topics are you writing about, what are you working on, what's your expertise? As soon as you notice someone who is interested and inquiring, give a few more key facts, validate their interest and the overlap between you, and then exchange contact information so that you can talk about it in a more relaxed space when the conference is over.

FIVE BIG TIPS FOR SMALL TALK

1. SMILE

Go up to your target with a smile and casually look them in the eye. This eases any situation and shows that you come "in peace."

An open smile always works when you're actually laughing. Try imagining something funny and laugh to yourself for a moment. Your smile immediately becomes authentic and is optimally conveyed to your counterpart. Richard Branson always uses this strategy and smiles throughout conversations and interviews.

2. INTRO

No awkward pre-packaged sentences, no name dropping, no drivel like "Hey, I just noticed you, and I'd like to introduce myself. My name is…" You don't need to say any more, and you wouldn't want to hear more if someone introduced themselves like that. Nobody wants to hear what you can do, and who you know. If you want to make sure that their first impression is a good one, offer a nice compliment ("Good speech!" "Nice shoes!" And so on.) Compliments are recognized worldwide as small talk lubricants!

3. HANDSHAKE

Short, firm, good. No laying on of hands like with the Pope, no twisting like with a Kung Fu grip, no dead fish, and *please* no bad right-left fist-bump combo (it never works, anyway). Short, firm, good!

4. CREATE VALUE

You always must have something to give. You can't come to a party without a present! If you want to help, you can support and connect other people. Consider something like, "Hey, I've been looking at your XYZ, and I realize that I know someone who could definitely help you make it even better!" Give first, then take—if at all. Your time will come!

5. CONNECT

"I'm glad we met each other. Let's get together sometime!" Exchange business cards. Better yet, get the person's number and ring them immediately. That way, your contact info is saved right there for when you call them again. With this out of the way, your name will be displayed whenever you decide to contact each other, eliminating the prospect of the dreaded "sound barrier" on that first call. Of course, you might run into difficulties: the person may not have cards (or claims to be out), not want to give out their number, or not be able to talk because they're busy leaving the building. If that's the case, then ask for someone on their team who you can contact. Come away from the event with at least some contact from the periphery of your target.

EXIT

"It's getting kind of late; I think I'll be off!" No, that's not true! Don't use an embarrassing farewell for your departure; it could ruin all of your preliminary work. Instead, do something smooth, nice, and honest, like "I'm going to go on another round of the room; will you be here later? It was really nice to meet you. Have a nice evening and see you soon!"

THE FOLLOW-UP

Your follow-up should take place fourteen days after your meeting—at the earliest. (After fourteen days, the waves made by the trade show should be settled.) It's best to store a reminder on your mobile phone, along with one or two reference points from your conversation.

The best time to send this first message is on a Tuesday afternoon, around 3:00 p.m. This ensures that the emails from the weekend have been processed, and that they're also finished with the emails from that morning. By the time you call, the person's inbox should be clean and their mood neutral. This is when your follow-up can produce the highest opening rate and the most impact. "Our Conversation" is always a good subject line since it make it clear that you already know each other from a face-to-face—even if your name no longer rings a bell.

Small talk should be fun. Go out and have fun, and never forget that everyone is glad to be approached in a nice way! Okay, I know for a fact some people will wonder "Okay, Matthew, does this also work with dating?" You are reading a book about business and life, so I suppose that you could argue that I owe you at least a few lines about dating. And hey, maybe something great will come along. You never know. Good luck and have fun!

DATING

(I have to smile as I write this word in my business book.) A short disclaimer: I don't see what follows as pick-up stuff or anything like that, but as a thought-provoking exercise for getting to know other people better—essentially, as a productivity shortcut for social contacts. What you make of it is your thing. (By the way, many of these thoughts don't come from a creepy dating coach, but from computer hacker Samy Kamkar, who was responsible for the MySpace virus "Samy," among other curiosities. This virus spread faster than any virus had before. But Samy also founded the Fonality startup at age seventeen, which was financed with $46 million. Cool guy. Google him!)

See yourself as a product in the market! How would you approach dating if you were marketing a product? There are dozens of books on the subject, but in the age of online dating and shortened communication channels, there's a lot we can optimize.

TEST YOUR PHOTOS

If we assume your aim is to get to know people online (though I'd advise you to explore people in real life—old-school style), then the first step starts with the picture/image—just like with products. Take three of your favorite pictures of yourself, contact ten people for comments on each photo, and note the conversion rate (the number of responses). That way you can tell which photos (regardless of your personal preference) are best accepted in the market.

TEST YOUR "SALES COPY"

What SMS texts, email subject lines, and chat mechanisms will give you your desired results? Write down what works (and what doesn't) and conceptualize the optimized "sales copy." It certainly sounds funny, but copy writing is an actual, highly paid profession (think of all the advertisements you've seen, and which ones have stuck). In the dating world, you are your own copy writer. And it's crazy to assume that you could "sell" something by using everyday blather like "Hey, how's it going...?" or "What's up?" Turn the scenario around. What if you got those uninspired messages? Would you return the call? Would you "buy"? No way! Those pitches are, quite frankly, pretty low effort. So change your approach! Tell me about yourself; ask about interesting things that evoke my positive emotions.

"What was your most interesting achievement this week?" Great question! If you're asked that, you have to think about great things, you feel good, and you know that someone is interested in what you feel.

SCARCITY

"Only five seats left." Have you ever seen this when booking a flight, for example? And what's the result? Panic and purchasing pressure. At the high-point of a conversation, one sentence in a phone call, chat, or SMS like, "Sorry, I have to go now, but maybe we can meet for coffee?" is strong, self-confident—and in a single moment, makes the offer scarce.

(As a side note, coffee is always better than dinner; it sounds less awkward and obligatory, and it's faster and cheaper. Who knows if this person you're meeting is a potential soul mate? If yes, then dinner will naturally follow. If not, you can be out of the coffee shop quicker and don't have to spend too much time or money on your "market analysis." Enjoy!)

By the way, you should always be honest and reveal your tactics and ideas at your first coffee. At worst, you'll have a funny conversation to talk about, and you won't feel like some comical pickup hacker.

5. WHAT DOES EXCELLENCE MEAN TO OUR TEAM?

We're at the starting line, everyone's in the mood and wants to do some excellent work, but what does that mean? It's essential to clearly communicate the expectations for the team's results—and together be aware of their significance. It poisons productivity when teams are not in the same boat regarding their principles and mission. Fear, uncertainty, and badly allocated resources (time/money) will infect every working team if everyone doesn't clearly understands the goal, the criteria by which the result will be measured, and the quality standards that this result should meet. Being afraid of the gap between expectations and outcomes always results in too little or too much thrust by the team, making it impossible to achieve a process-optimizing "middle ground." To create clarity and to set the framework, it's important for each leader to communicate the goal and the conditions must be met in order to have an "excellent" outcome. Ultimately, they must help the team clearly envision what the project will look like when it is finished.

It's very important to distinguish between excellence and perfection. No one is perfect or can produce perfect work. The demand for perfect results hinders the learning process and progress. The best of the best are not interested in perfection—they want to achieve excellence! They demand a high standard for themselves and—though they are by no means perfect—always perform beyond the status quo, always higher than expected. The pump is always primed.

People need visuals. What does a person you respect look like? What inspires you about this person and why? What exactly does excellence look like in their lives? Understanding this precisely will enable you to make better decisions. Better decisions and your own concept of excellence will lead to better results. What would your life look like if you really imposed that standard on yourself? Where would you be personally and professionally, and how would you feel? When you really grow personally, you feel good. You don't waste your talents. The team exists at its highest level. You live the life you deserve and owe to yourself. Respect and energy result from your best work and from the true excellence in you and in your team! A clear picture creates a clear perspective, and clear perspectives smooth even the most impassable of paths.

SOME IDEAS FOR GREAT PERSPECTIVES

- Have we produced a high-quality product (measured by market standards) that solves our customers' problems? Is the entire team proud to stand behind this product? Can I sign off on this product with my name, and recommend it in complete earnestness?

- Did we follow a high-quality (measured by our values) interpersonal process while producing this product? It's not only about the quality of the outcome, and not only about the goal, but also about the path and the people on this path. Has our team grown with this product? Have we honored all the people who've been involved?

- Have we respected our mission? A quality product and a solid process are worthless if the result does not represent the values, principles, and the "Why" of your team. The foundation of the team, the structure that enables every company to exist, is built on a belief, a conviction, and a very specific idea that is shared by everyone in the company. In order to be "excellent," every product that leaves your shop must be consistent with this conviction.

Ask yourself the above three questions whenever your team starts a new project. And when you finish, highlight the results by using the three to assess measuring your true excellence. Always involve your team in the feedback round!

Decide together what good work means to you, so that each individual knows exactly what to do in order to make an effective, productive, and fulfilling contribution to the team in the long term.

At this point, I assume that the values and principles are part of the team and can be relied upon. If not, take three steps back, sit down with your team, and workout the following five questions together.

The result should be written down and displayed in a special place in the office for all to see.

- What are our values, and what do we stand for as a team?
- Why do we work together every day?
- How do we deal with each other?
- What is our common goal?
- Besides using it in our work, how can we use our strength as a team?

These basic values will be your anchor, both in good times and bad. No matter what happens, you can always refer back to them—remember what they really are. These basic values are also your compass; with them, you and your team will never get lost. It's all about working as a team to do really breathtaking work, and about knowing exactly what that means. Everything your team does every day should be consistent with your values and with your understanding of excellence, and this daily work should fulfill everyone.

6. FLYING WITHOUT TAKING OFF

Every reflective leader repeatedly asks themselves the question: "Do I seem arrogant right now?" It's a necessary question for everyone who stands in front, who shows others the way, who tells them where to go. How do you become a calm leader whose success is acknowledged everywhere? How can you make yourself clearly visible, but without showing off? Don't concentrate on the beauty of the flowers, but on the roots that feed them! Here are some practical ways you can lead people while still staying grounded.

HONESTY AND AUTHENTICITY

When you are truly yourself, you never run the risk of appearing arrogant. Arrogance stems from an artificial façade that you create under pressure and with little reflection. It's a role you play, an instrument you use to amplify elements of yourself, your abilities, and your achievements. This technique is never natural, and it definitely doesn't work if you have based your leadership principles on honesty and authenticity.

BE ACCESSIBLE

Inaccessibility creates distance, and distance always seems arrogant and unsympathetic. Leaders who are not approachable suggest a class-based system that poisons the mood in the team. As long as you remain approachable, open-minded, helpful, and understanding, you will remain emotionally at eye level with your team. As long as someone can feel your warmth, you are among the people. A tip: look others in the eyes, be reachable, physically engage with your conversation partner (for example, by a touch on the shoulder), and always try to understand and respect their perspectives.

TALK ABOUT THE POSITIVES

Unfortunately, ineffective leaders always see themselves as firefighters. If it's burning, they come to extinguish it. If something goes wrong, they sound the alarms. But what's more interesting is the leader who's there when nothing is on fire, who applauds when things are going well. Remind your team of the beauty of the sun's rays, celebrate the positives, and rejoice in the small victories. In a punitive culture, there are only the "normal" and "shitstorm" modes. Find the middle and be a leader whose feelings of pride and joy are visible to his team. This healthier balance makes any constructive criticism much more effective because the people are expecting positivity.

YOUR TEAM IS YOUR CATHEDRAL!

SUCCESS IS ALWAYS A PRODUCT OF THE TEAM

Only a weak leader repeatedly refers to "his" successes. Remove yourself. Everyone knows you're the leader—you don't have to remind them. Of course, if you've scored a lot of Big Points, that's great! That's actually what's expected of you. But what's much more important is your job as a role model. As a leader, you don't just lead a team; you introduce new leaders to their role as captains. They should become like you. Leaders build people up without needing to hear applause for doing so.

The applause you want is when the team succeeds. You made the important passes in the midfield, sure, but the whole team scored the goal. Let the team cheer and dance as the points rack up, and rejoice quietly about the spotlight you were able to provide them. Be a play-maker and a game-player, and your team and the whole stadium will love you for it.

BE AN ARCHITECT OF COLLABORATION

Connect rooms, floors, buildings, and wings. Design stairs and corridors, doors, and gates. Create entrances and elevators, basements and storage. Your designs are open, spacious, thoughtful, and beautiful. Unite people and emotions, talents and skills. Create bridges and tunnels. Bring hands together that must find each other, build structures that are indestructibly stable and tower up to the sky. Your buildings will still stand hundreds of years from now because they are built upon the principles of a real leader. Standing on a stable foundation, the beams and columns of your art combine to form a seemingly complex vault of strength and synergy. Your team is your cathedral.

MONEY AND HAPPINESS

I pointed out in another chapter that the old saying "Money can't buy happiness" is not completely true because money and financial independence make many things easier and enable people to own and experience wonderful things. But while money can sure make life more manageable, it's actually a proven—and a fundamental—concept that there is no direct correlation between happiness and money.

I'd like to call in a colleague who can make this point truly irrefutable!

The so-called Easterlin Paradox examines the potential connection between money and happiness. It was first introduced in 1974 by economist Richard Easterlin in his essay "Does Economic Growth Improve the Human Lot?" Easterlin had studied people in various countries and cultures who had just earned significantly more money than usual (salary increases, bonuses, etc.), and found the same results across the board: as long as people's basic needs are met, more money does not automatically mean more happiness.

People very quickly adapt a new standard of living to their new incomes. Their fires are usually burning no brighter at the end of the month as they were before. With the change in pay, there's also usually a change in purchasing behavior. People think they need things that can communicate their prosperity to their neighbors. The resulting yardsticks and pressures put entire (usually rich) neighborhoods in financial difficulty. Everybody has to drive an expensive car, play golf, and put their kids through private school. Not everyone really can, but it seems like everyone has to try.

What happens is a distortion of wealth and income. It turns into the expression of wealth per dollar earned. Let's consider how personal finances are allocated in terms of productivity and efficiency. In my opinion, those who can convert their income into prosperity through long-term investments are the ones who are truly rich (especially in terms of foresight). However, that style of money management only works if you don't care what your neighbor thinks about your car (which otherwise might have to be expensively leased, negatively affecting your income/wealth factor in order to "look rich.") The one who has the courage to resist the current is both truly free *and* smart!

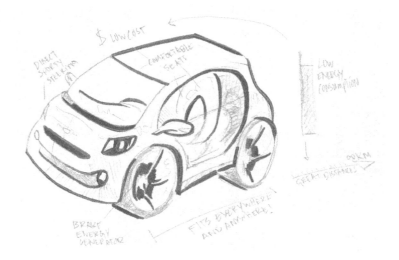

QUICK TIP

I drive a Smart car. I purchased it used, but it was less than one year old. I didn't purchase it because there was no other option for me, but because it really made sense. It was economical in the purchase price, fuel consumption, and taxes. I can find a parking place anywhere, and don't have to give everyone a ride as there are only two seats. My car is a tool to get me from point A to point B as efficiently as possible. If you buy your car as a status symbol to impress your neighbor, you won't be happy (there's always a more expensive, faster car) and you'll burn through money unnecessarily. Be smart! A tool must make sense. After all, we don't install nails with a diamond hammer.

The media helps encourage enormous misunderstandings about the buying behavior of wealthy people. We think rich people always have expensive things. Wrong—if so, they'd exhaust their funds and would not be rich! (Well, at least not sustainably.) In terms of cost-benefit ratio, wealthy people are statistically proven to be more economical than the middle class. The car most purchased by millionaires is not a Porsche, but most likely a used Ford or a Toyota—a lot of car for little money. A new car loses 20 to 30 percent of its value in the first year. (If this depreciation is optimally leveraged, you get a really good deal.) You don't become a millionaire through luck, but through conscious purchasing decisions that make sense.

According to Dr. Thomas Stanley, author of the authoritative *Stop Acting Rich* (an absolute must-read), the clear pioneer in this group of foxes is the engineer. In his book, Stanley compares the typical myths about wealthy people with the reality of their often very down-to-earth way of doing business. He writes that engineers are, by far, the craftiest and most economical occupational group. It's all about their unique analytical way of thinking. They are oriented toward problem solving and getting results that are reproducible in the long term, results that are useful and logical. Just like they use complex thought processes to produce physical objects, engineers also use the laws of nature to their own advantage. Their approach to the market is "counter-cyclic." (Brilliant. Try it!) For example, I bought my snowboarding equipment in July for 70 percent less than I would have paid in November. I also book my holidays early or very last-minute, always outside the busy season, and to places that are not yet mainstream.

Invest when everyone is selling, sell when everyone is buying, drive to work earlier to avoid rush hour, go to IKEA on Wednesday at noon. Think through your route in advance and be where no one else is. Brave and smart, logical and calculating—become the engineer of your everyday life and your financial planning!

At best, material purchases trigger a brief adrenalin rush, but will never provide lasting pleasure. It's more important to orient your professional life toward real meaning and significance, rather than toward potential monetary results. You're happy when you live your best life, not when you make more money. Increase your value without spending it away, and financial independence will follow. But money without meaning is a nosedive!

7. SPEAKING (YES, IN FRONT OF GROUPS)

"There are people who'd rather die than speak in front of a group!" Have you heard this before? Incredible, isn't it? There apparently are people who'd prefer to end their life in order to escape presenting in front of a group. If you're thinking, "Well, I also don't really like speaking in front of a group," I have an important message for you. You are reading a book that I have written for people who want to change something, who want to grow beyond themselves, who want to generate ideas, and who want to challenge the status quo. Because you're not satisfied with what's being offered. You want more! And if this "more" does not yet exist, you'll develop and implement it. This talent is a gift that you owe to your environment. The people around you have to hear about it, have to see it, and have to want to be lifted up by you. As long as you refuse to stand and speak in front of the group (symbolizing the world that wants to receive your gift), you are doing yourself and your environment a great injustice. You are denying those around you the opportunity to share in your gift, in your creativity, and in your higher purpose. At the same time, you also take away your chance to prove to yourself what you can do.

Imagine if you'd never started riding a bike. Certainly not a big problem, but your speed, efficiency, sense of achievement, and the resulting miles that you can easily travel on your bike for the rest of your life—all that would not exist. You wouldn't miss them because you wouldn't know what you were giving up, but a whole part of your life would remain unwritten.

It's exactly the same with speaking. Of course, at first it's uncomfortable. That's the same for everyone, including me. The adrenaline that's released when the spotlight comes on, finding yourself the focus of the audience's undivided attention—both create pressure, no question. But just alter the scene. Don't tell yourself, "Oh man, this place is full! Everybody's here, I'm shaking, I can hardly breathe, everything's cramping up. I'm trapped!" Instead, tell yourself, "Oh man, this place is full! Everybody's here, I'm shaking, I can hardly breathe, everything's cramping up. Now I'm ready!" Your greatest fear is your greatest opportunity for growth. The opportunity arrives so that you can take the experience with you. Go with it!

For those who are still hesitant, here are a few time-tested tips that help me before every big presentation and before every speech that I'm invited to give for big companies or conventions:

- **Fear is growth.** When your fear is the greatest, you are ready!

- **Preparation is everything.** Anyone who says you can always wing it has never given a clean, concentrated presentation. Learn every word, take your time, be disciplined, and enjoy the gift of serenity that comes after the chaos of preparation.

- **Build bridges!** Use keywords, mnemonic devices, and mental connections. Think in pictures and stories, and really understand your content so that you can "bring your presentation to life." It's not enough to simply speak the words. The words must flow without you thinking about them. Become the content yourself, live the message, play with the message, and you'll fly through your speech.

- **Tell stories!** People love stories, so give them what they love. Pack the most complex relationships into stories from life, into real observations, and into content that is transferable to the listener. Those who recognize themselves will become part of the story, no matter what the content is.

- **Be real!** On stage, don't even try to be somebody else—they'll notice that immediately. Go out, be real, and people will love you for it!

- **The audience is on your side.** Everyone in the audience wants you to succeed. The listeners respect the fact that you are standing up there and want to give them something. (Certainly some would rather die than trade places with you.) They're your fans simply because you're on stage. These people support you—enjoy it and don't be afraid!

- **Connect!** Go through the rows before your presentation and introduce yourself, wish people lots of fun, look into their eyes, shake hands! This takes away fear from both you and them, and your speech becomes a relaxed conversation among friends. You have no problem speaking to your family at the dining table.

- **Give them something!** Be aware that everyone in the audience must take away something from your presentation: a sentence, a keyword, a central message. Define this beforehand and put it in your head so that it becomes unforgettable!

I can honestly say that speaking in front of a group has been one of the most important building blocks in my development as a person and as a businessman. To face one's own fear and to share one's gift is an indescribable feeling!

I want everyone to have the same feeling and would be happy to help you on your way to becoming a speaker. Visit my Mockridge School of Leadership (www.matthewmockridge.com).

8. EYES ON THE ROAD

Watch the road closely, especially if you are successful! If successful (financially, personally, with a karate black belt, or otherwise well on your way), then you're probably thinking "Boy, it's going well with me! What do you have to teach me?" Exactly this: If it's working, it's really going well, everything you touch turns to gold, and colorful confetti rains down on your belly of prosperity—then that's exactly when it becomes very dangerous! When you're flying at 130 miles per hour over the highway, you won't be concentrating on the road. You'll be talking, making phone calls, waving to the right, waving to the left, looking out the window, forgetting how careful you were in the early days. Everything is going great, the music is playing—and then there's a *bang*!

It happened all of a sudden, out of nowhere. Everything was going so well. Nobody saw it coming. I've heard so many people say after a disaster that "Basically, everything was okay. It was going great!" It becomes truly dangerous when you're really successful. Arrogance, laziness, comfort. You stop fighting, you stop striving, and you're complacent.

Keep your eyes on the road, especially when everything starts moving really fast. And that applies to everyone! Everyone in the company, everyone on the team. Board members, managing directors, owners, managers, trainees, interns—everyone! Stay hungry, keep reaching for the stars. You must really want something, stand for something, and want to control your destiny (a.k.a. your car) consciously and with a clear goal, every day! Keep your eyes on the road, especially when the scenery speeding by makes the route seem so easy. Stay cool, stay modest, stay yourself! Transfer this mindset to all areas of your life! Never forget where you started from. Reach for the stars with your business, but also with your family and with your community.

A job is just a job if you choose to see it as just a job. My grandmother used to say, "Every job is noble, as long as you do it with all your heart." A beautiful thought! No matter what you do, the fulfillment and value of your work depend on the choices you make every second on the playing field of your life and job. Take out the garbage on Monday morning the same way Michelangelo painted. Every job is a chance to face the things that frighten you so that you can grow. Every job is an opportunity to promote your values to your team and your clients. No matter what you do, never stop striving, no matter how successful you become. Because you—not your success—set the pace! You can inspire people from the first to the last day of your life, give hope to the hopeless, and give it everything you've got. Success is a by-product that gives you freedom, but it must never slow you down. Every day that you are passionate for your work is a chance to change the world!

With all due respect and with great care, I want to ask something from you, my friend: Please never forget the inner fire of the beginner that made you successful in the first place! Stay more creative, better, faster, and more innovative than everyone else. Never feel "safe." Stay sharp! The biggest risk is a life without risk. When things are going better, listen better! When you get really good at something, learn more! Each new day is an opportunity to learn something grow, no matter what happened yesterday.

The clockwork of your success turns in the opposite direction from the wheels of your character. The more successful you become, the more humble you must become.

9. WHY LEADERS EAT LAST

In the US military, there's a defined order in which food is eaten: the youngest eat first, and the highest eat last. The leader symbolically sacrifices himself for the team, so that the team will sacrifice itself in the field for him. The leader is the one who takes the first step and is the first to make a sacrifice. He sets an example for what he demands from his team.

I hear and see again and again the distorted image of the type of leader who only enjoys and exploits his status—the typical villain in every movie. This idea of a leader—one who doesn't lead, but just lets things happen, who doesn't give but just takes, who enjoys but doesn't share—is unthinkable in reality. The so-called "stupid boss" either reflects the fevered imagination of a sick team or represents a really weak leader. Frustration and disrespect decrease the raison d'être of any leader who incorrectly carries out their duties, and evokes those same emotions in their team. Anyone who rose to the top via "connections"—family or otherwise—will have their inadequacies noticed immediately. A leader makes their own way upwards and is not led there through the back door.

People need security. Business is on the front line. There's a war raging, involving the competition, insecurity, fear, and one's own will. Markets and competitors are uncontrollable. The only control we have is the culture within our company, within our team.

When people feel safe and know that the leader wants what's best for the team and that he will be the last to eat, they will react with trust and cooperation. Only then will people give their all to jointly overcome the danger and uncontrollability that's outside, on the front line. Fear of the unknown always requires a supporting pillar—a leader who sacrifices himself. Fear of the unknown, fear of each other, and fear of one's own ranks can make the strongest teams implode. If people think that the leader puts results ahead of the team or if the leader will only eat last if the performance was good, the cooperative mood reverts to a fear for survival.

In the face of fear, people spend their energy protecting themselves. Inefficiency contaminates the team. Fear correlates with weakness.

Think about yourself: How do you feel about the people you work with? How do they treat you? When you are confronted humanly, you do the same. Remember, only people can be human, so always separate people and emotions from numbers and facts. For the leader, it's a key skill to be able to see the human being. What people form your team? Who are your customers? When your customers become human, your decisions become better, and you immediately, by degrees, become more responsible, ethical and moral. When people represent nothing but numbers, your decisions are weak. Weak leaders never see people. They see the big company, the "bad" boss. When you stop seeing the person, everyone tries to cheat. In a weak culture among weak leaders, people don't do the right thing for the team; they do the right thing for themselves.

The leader who eats first seeks the advantage for themselves. The leader who eats last shows trust, honesty, loyalty, and empathy. When these emotions are in front of the team, the team reacts with the same emotion. People react honestly to honesty. People react to manipulation with manipulation. This is a law of nature and the human urge to survive. Those who think they are getting too small a slice of the pie will only work for themselves; any cooperation goes down the drain. When people have little, but they stick together and their emotions are healthy, they will help each other. Unfortunately, the opposite is problematic, because when people have too much, the value is diminished. If we receive too much, we protect our nest. This seems paradoxical, but it's reality. In the poorest areas of the world, where emotions are healthy, people help each other. In the world's richest neighborhoods, people hide behind high walls and alarm systems. Selfishness. They are no longer approachable—physically or psychologically. Without a doubt, there are many very wealthy people in the world who give a lot, but it is in the nature of humans (when they are doing well) to share little and to hoard a lot.

It's important to always have great visions. These dreams keep you hungry and prevent you from walling yourself in with your current treasure, like a weak leader hiding behind his selfish fear of loss. No matter how much we have, we should always have more hunger. Not because we are not full, but because the gift we have to give is so much greater. We cannot leave our potential untapped. We are still at the back of the food line, but the queue is getting longer and the crew is getting hungrier. That driving force is a strong "Why."

There has to be a grand vision that stands above everything, including every leader. Every entrepreneur has a big vision at the beginning, nothing else. If you become successful, the vision becomes reality, and your goals have now become too small. But the vision must be greater than the means so that it always remains stronger than the hunger. With this star above and up ahead, comrades fearlessly advance daily into any uncertainty. They know that this common effort is about something very special. We are all part of this story; we are writing it together. The pen is only briefly put aside when everyone strengthens themselves in the safety of peace and tranquility. But the leader eats last!

10. LEADERS FOLLOWERS = EXPONENTIAL GROWTH

Not everyone is a leader; the world needs both leaders and followers alike. Only when one follows does it make sense for someone else to lead. Followers are the supporting walls of the house, indispensably important and essential. Good leaders need followers that are just as good. The product of leaders and followers is exponential growth. As long as the leader continues to develop new leaders out of the pool of followers, the group continues to grow stronger—over and over again!

On their teams, leaders see more than people. They see potential; they recognize the leaders of tomorrow, the still uncut rough diamonds. Have you ever noticed someone simply because they look strong, or because they moves differently, and stand out from the crowd? You feel it immediately—this person has a completely different energy. The ability to recognize potential is a gift. To promote it is a gift. However, to push it beyond oneself is the act of a master. Good leaders notice another selfless image. They see people and situations with completely different eyes. The eyes of a hero always see a different picture than the eyes of a victim, even if on the surface the two seem identical.

PERSPECTIVE OF THE VICTIM

The victim sees problems, precisely identifies obstacles, classifies the danger, imagines the degree of difficulty, defines the risk, and receives validation from society and those around him. The victim argues shrewdly and glibly, with phrases like "That will never work!" The victim is comforted by the safe agreement of the majority: "Yes, you're right. That can't work!" Conventional thinking establishes a trend where everyone looks the same and everyone has the same limiting beliefs. Society carefully sets the bar just high enough so that everyone can somehow participate without stretching. Everything is relaxed, and everyone can play along.

PERSPECTIVE OF THE WILD WEST HERO

The hero sees a great opportunity in danger. It's not about risk-taking or stupidity, but about a basic attitude: when you have to strain, you build muscle. But with a generation that wraps itself in conformity and the supposed security of the group, the same type of job candidates (with the same faces and the same background stories) pass through the personnel departments and the executive floors. A herd of cows, driven in a circle. Whoever falls out of line stands alone—yet that's the only true position for the hero. A herd has direction, an idea, a model, some sort of guidelines. But outside the herd is the Wild West. Outside the herd, a rocky unchartered path rewards courageous cowboys who dare to follow it with endless views of the most beautiful canyons. He sees sights no one else has seen before.

Out there, new worlds are opening up. Out there, heroes are born whose stories of fearlessness and great successes circulate among the herds and inspire them to keep running. If we just keep going, something has to happen. We can do it. Movement, not freedom.

Break away from the herd and go the other way, to where no one has been before! Do something new, expose yourself to danger, and the infinity of the prairie will inspire you to overcome adversity. While the herd walks around in circles, you will climb the mountain! The views from below and from above are both in the hero's perspective. It's all about the path and the result, again and again.

PERSPECTIVE OF THE HERO IN AN OFFICE

The hero doesn't see a desk, he sees a blank canvas. His work is an unfinished masterpiece. This isn't about money; this is about the conviction to give his best! You will be rewarded like those in the top 1 percent if you do what only the top 1 percent is willing to do. Pride is the voice in you that confirms that you have given your best. This voice never lies—it's your bio-feedback, the voice of nature, the voice of your soul, the voice of your heart. If you don't give everything you've got, your pride will come and try to take away your sense of respect, for she is hungry, and that is good. If you don't give your best to her, she'll turn away from you and start to distance herself. As long as you don't accept and tolerate your pride, as long as you don't listen to her voice within you, the distance between you and your pride becomes bigger, and the pain becomes more intense. The distance between you and your pride correlates with the intensity of your inner conflict. Your pride is always right, knows exactly what you can do, and knows what you are capable of. Every day, the struggle rages between pride and stubbornness, between heart and head, between passion and lethargy. So promise yourself that you will always be very close to your pride. Listen to her voice inside you and let her lead you to unimaginable places and the fantastic realms of fulfillment and happiness. Go where your pride takes you. Take the blank canvas, and don't just paint to finish it (we're not in eighth grade art class)—paint to create a masterpiece! Start something today! Do something today for which your future self will be grateful!

PERSPECTIVE OF THE HERO IN SPORTS

Change is uncomfortable, training is hard, and perfecting skills takes years. But the chaos of helplessness and the exhaustion of strength and will are always followed by clarity and blessing. Your 400-meter sprint of change is uncomfortable at the beginning, so you are full of fear. Halfway through the track, it's chaotic and uncontrolled, but once you've crossed the finish line, a dream of clarity, fulfillment, and freedom awaits. So, just keep running!

PERSPECTIVE OF THE HERO AT A CONVEYOR BELT

All day long, we are confronted with distractions. The conveyor belt of life is full and running around the clock at top speed. Your eye for the essentials is your secret weapon. You reach purposefully toward the full conveyor belt, again and again, and pull out exactly what you are looking for. Distractions are deadly on the conveyor belt of life—the complexity and confusion, the volume and distractions, the temptation to let your gaze wander again and again. But the hero remains focused, understanding that concentration and reduction control everything. A clear gaze, a quick grasp: You get what you need, and the rest of the garbage just goes past you, unnoticed, and untouched. Your eyes see only that which moves you forward; everything else is in motion toward you or away from you.

PERSPECTIVE OF THE HERO IN THE MORNING

It's not the coffee that wakes you up, *you* wake yourself up! Heroes understand where their deepest energy originates. Deep inside you rests the power to propel everything, to kick start everything, and to celebrate every victory! No external influence can transfer to you the power that you can give to yourself. Real power emanates inwardly, never outwardly. No drug, no surroundings, no sun, no person will be able to trigger in you what you can develop in yourself. When you decide to wake yourself up, to take the first step yourself, to apply the energy yourself, then your pride immediately rewards you: even more motivation will arise that will drive you to develop new energy within, which in turn will lead you to more motivation. You are now in an endless energy-motivation cycle, and you can achieve anything you want. Increased self-confidence now makes you stronger! Your whole being changes—mentally and physically—and with every new day, you rise higher in the spiral of energy and trust!

PERSPECTIVE OF THE HERO IN A TEAM

Heroes know exactly this: action is everything. A good plan at this moment is better than a brilliant plan in two months, when it's too late. The fast ones eat the slow ones. Step on the gas and take action! The bigger your goals, the more important the team becomes. Teamwork makes the dream work! You can eat less of a big pie than you can a small one. Not only will the big one taste better, but the joy and fulfillment of eating and sharing with the team will completely overshadow any other dessert. Influence your team by your good example and lead each individual to success. The hero turns the weaker person into a hero, and then steps out of the spotlight themselves. The hero doesn't stand around talking, but lets actions speak for themselves. On the hero's team, anyone who really makes a difference can also be a hero. Even if team members make mistakes, the hero is satisfied, because the only real mistake on the hero's team is the mistake of not trying.

PERSPECTIVE OF THE HERO IN A CIRCLE OF FRIENDS

Heroes surround themselves with other heroes who inspire, promote, challenge, encourage, push, and help! Heroes always have their own heroes, people they look up to whose routines, attitudes, ideas, and lives they emulate. Heroes know they have to learn every day. The hero immediately sees whether things are helping him or slowing him down. The perspectives of the big picture, the long journey, and the important path shape the focus of the hero. In the preliminary round, he already sees the finals—he sees the victory from the very first minute. It's not about individual moves, not about the balls or the goals lost, it's about the victory at the end! The hero never loses sight of this victory. Heroes create worlds that inspire and help deliver world-class performance, every time. Heroes give more than they want to receive. They create value for as many people as possible. The hero's question is "How can I help a million people?"—not "How can I get a million dollars?" Giving is the start of an automated process that ensures that you get something. Only those who give get something back!

PERSPECTIVE OF THE SAD

People eat junk food because they feel so much deep pain and so much inner turmoil, that the fulfillment and numbness of unhealthy food is their only consolation.

This instant consolation becomes a pattern, a ritual. The body is poisoned, one's happiness and one's pride become more and more distant, and the desire for consolation becomes ever greater. Consolation becomes a model of life. A vicious circle of disappointment and false consolation leads to even more grief, creating an endless negative spiral that leads you down into the deep cellar of your personal misfortune, which becomes harder to leave every day.

Your potential best life watches, deeply troubled by how poorly you handle the gift of each new day. Even if you want to forget or hide what you are doing, your best life sees everything and cries every tear with you. The root of real misfortune lies in the betrayal of your authenticity, which could have led you to unimaginable places. Looking back and not knowing what you could have been is the ultimate pain.

Why do people eat unhealthy food? Why do they make fun of others? Why do they gloat? Why are they unhappy? Because they are in pain. The pain is about the gap between their potential and their reality. Pain about feeling the distance between their hopes and what they have achieved. And the moments in which these people can break away from their pain, are the moments in which they try to raise themselves above others, physically or verbally. In those moments, they live excessively, eat too much, drink too much, take too many drugs, and "consume" too much sex. "High" on adrenaline and power, those are the moments during which they can briefly forget their pain. For a brief moment, they are invincible because they feel they are in control. But in truth, they have only transferred control to the substances of their choice and have plunged head over heels into addiction—the next morning the game starts all over again.

In this type of state, you don't see the world as it really is, but through the filters of your philosophy. You see the world from the perspective you believe in and from the perspectives offered by those around you. If your parents, your friends, your boss or teacher, the newspaper, bestow their beliefs upon you with a perspective of mediocrity, you become: mediocre! It's that simple. Every person sees the world a little differently. Each perspective focuses on different elements; each story is different and casts a different light on each scene in your very own world. Your conscience is the jury.

Don't try to change the world. Instead, change your perspective, change your story, control the way you illuminate your outlook, and your world will change instantly. Not having what you want does not mean that you really aren't able to get it. Instead, it means that your story and your perspective have suggested to you that you don't deserve it, or that you can't reach it, or that you can't afford it!

The good news is that you pay for happiness with a currency that you can print yourself. *You* alone decide the currency in which you want to pay! The price for your happiness is your very own contribution. How much are you willing to give? How much are you willing to train? You will be able to pay the seemingly unaffordable cost of happiness and get "rich" when you step on the gas and focus on the few things that are essential for your success. You know exactly what to do (the Winner's Routine). Do it, and you'll be rich in happiness. Don't do it, and the account balance of your happiness will be overdrawn. Your deposit was too little, your withdrawal too much, and you sink deep into the red. You can't exist like that!

The moment that your courage, your work, your will, and your determination weigh less than what it takes to make you happy, you become emotionally insolvent. Always pay into your happiness account, every day, and only withdraw some when you really deserve it. No shortcuts! Victims always want everything faster, better, and with as little effort as possible. Where is the patience? The fantasy of a Happiness Pill is a fairy tale. Without input, there can be no output. Everybody sees the result, but nobody sees the path to get there. Everybody wants to skip the marathon and still win a medal. That won't work!

TEAMWORK MAKES THE DREAM WORK!

Afterword

Congrats, friend!

As you read these lines, I want to make it very clear how much I respect and appreciate you: I'm truly a fan of yours! People tend to read books (if they read them at all) only in bits and pieces, starting, stopping, and usually don't make it all the way to the end—like with so many other things in life. The path of least resistance becomes the ordinary route, and an ordinary existence becomes everyday life.

Seeing things through to the end is the Holy Grail, the singular mystery of life, and the big difference. When your eyes are ready for your brilliance, they suddenly see things that were previously invisible. That time has now come. People are fascinated by results, not by processes. They don't see the whole truth. It's about the final, winning shot, not the entire game before it; it's about the great body, not the years of training; it's about the big sale, not the rocky road that led to it. Why are investment scams, "get rich quick" schemes, gambling, and the lottery always so effectively tempting? People focus too much on results! Ever since humans have existed, wealth and success have fascinated us—but mainly just the goal, not the journey!

Now that you've finished this entire book, respected the process, and taken the journey upon yourself (despite the temptations of the mainstream and against all odds), you understand what this book was all about: the process. Every single page of this book is about developing a life based on strong processes, on an unshakable foundation, on values, and on your unique journey. If you truly understand that, then I promise you something: you'll never have to worry about your results again! They will surpass your wildest dreams!

This book promises a result. Just look at the title. On the surface, our encounter was all about the result—the big idea. Why? Because people want results. The title maximizes the number of hands that will hold this book—it's my chance to explain the importance of the process to as many people as possible who want results. So, it's a book about the process, about the thoughts that generate real success and make happiness possible—all dressed up in an attractively easy format, optimized for fast results.

It's my true desire and greatest goal that you read these lines and understand the great circle that this book is now closing. The path, each new step, every new second in which you choose your best authentic life—that is the all-important idea!

If you understand this and sense the value of this journey, then do what I do: Use the power of the book's title to find the great path that is hidden behind the simple steps. Give this book to someone who needs to know about it, who needs it, and who will understand it. Give this book to someone who will be honestly grateful to you for really believing in them and their way!

I hope you will always look back with a smile, pride, and joy on the hours we both spent together with this book—I sure do!

I wish you only the best from the bottom of my heart. I respect you and thank you sincerely for your trust.

And I'd really love to hear from you and your journey!

Thank you,
YOUR FAN, MATTHEW

Thank You!

Unbelievable! As I write these lines, I'm filled with a deep sense of joy and pride—a broad, honest smile on my face. My first book is finished! A project from my heart that has been with me every day for over two years. Even if it's only my name on the cover, there are some people without whom this book never would have been written. I'd like to express my special thanks to the following people.

To my wonderful wife Sarah-Lia: I love you; you're a gift to the world! Little Ava, you're a miracle!

To my family: Love you all in our crazy Mockridge way!

To my co-founders: What a run! Thanks for making this whole story happen.

Many thanks to my buddy Dr. Stefan Frädrich: Dear Stefan, your open arms got the ball rolling!

To GABAL VERLAG and to Mango:

Many thanks to the whole team for your help and great cooperation! Dear Ute, you are my "partner in crime." We did it! Thanks for your trust!

TO YOU:

From the bottom of my heart, I would like to thank you, last but not least! You hold this book in your hands and make all of this possible! Only through your interest, your curiosity, your growth, your joy in learning, and through this moment do I have the chance to share my story and my thoughts to help you and other people realize your dreams and theirs. For this, I am eternally grateful to you!

LOVE, MATTHEW

About the Author

Matthew Mockridge studied international business and management at Florida International University in Miami, Florida, USA. He is a serial entrepreneur, a bestselling author, an official coach to the contestants in the primetime TV show START-UP!, and an international keynote speaker for companies such as Philips, Sony Pictures Television, Lufthansa, RE/MAX, and many more.

www.matthewmockridge.com